CROCHET *in a* DAY

CROCHET *in a* DAY

18 Easy Patterns for Cute Sweaters, Cozy Blankets, Stylish Shawls and More

ANGIE BIVINS

**Creator of
Whistle and Wool**

PAGE STREET
PUBLISHING CO.

PAGE STREET
PUBLISHING CO.

First published in 2024 by
Page Street Publishing Co.
27 Congress Street, Suite 1511
Salem, MA 01970
www.pagestreetpublishing.com

Distributed by Macmillan, sales in Canada by The Canadian Manda Group.

28 27 26 25 24   1 2 3 4 5

ISBN-13: 979-8-89003-107-5

Library of Congress Control Number: 2023949686

Edited by Erica Chamberlain
Cover and book design by Laura Benton for Page Street Publishing Co.
Photography by Stephen and Angie Bivins

Printed and bound in China

To my mum, who always taught
me to check my tension.

I miss you.

TABLE *of* CONTENTS

Quick but Comfy Cardigans   29

Dune Vest   31
A chunky vest with all the coziness you need in a knit look!

Coastal Cardigan   37
An oversized cardigan with tons of comfort, a cozy collar and pockets!

Embrace Cardigan   45
A cute button-up cardigan with lots of texture and a cuffed sleeve detail

Sway Sweater   55
An oversized cropped sweater with a flowy texture and easy neck shaping

Wrapped in Warmth Shawls + Wraps   61

Shelter Shawl   63
An open textured wrap worked up in bulky yarn for the colder months

Yesterday Wrap   69
A nostalgic, granny-stitched square texture with modern shaping for endless color combos

In a Jiffy Scarf   75
An extra-long scarf with an open texture for easy draping

INTRODUCTION

Few things are as good as the feeling you get when you start and complete a project on the same day. Each of these 18 cozy projects can be crocheted in just 24 hours or less, and they encompass everything from cute home details to oversized garments that will wrap you up in a big yarn hug.

When I designed all these adorable patterns, it was for all of us who love cozy garments and décor that work up quickly! I love a relaxing and simple project. With easy shaping and textured stitches, there's a pattern for all seasons and activities throughout the book. While these projects are simple to make and easy to work up, I've added cute details to each of the patterns so that the projects don't look basic when you're showing them off.

As you go through this book, you'll find a rough time estimate for each project. This means it took me and my testers approximately that much time to stitch at our normal pace. The hope is that these time references will help you plan how a project can fit into your day, week or month. Remember that timing can vary per yarn artist, so even if a shawl takes 5 to 5½ hours according to the book, that's just an estimate.

The great thing is that the patterns can be worked all in one sitting or broken up over a few days to accommodate your schedule. Say you have a last-minute gift to make by next week, and you like the 4-hour Marlo Tote (page 113) or the 6-hour Serene Throw (page 81). Sometimes you don't have a long, quiet day to dedicate to all that stitching, and things come up. By dedicating just an hour a day to crocheting, you'll get that 6-hour blanket done with time to spare! Projects take the amount of time they take, and budgeting your time can make your project easier to enjoy.

While all of the projects are easy to work up, some of the techniques may be new to you. For that, I have a library of stitch tutorials on my YouTube channel (Whistle and Wool) to help. Not all of the patterns in the book may be an ideal first-time project, so I recommend starting with a simple pattern like the Breezy Headband (page 129), and then when you are feeling confident, you can dive into something bigger like the Coastal Cardigan (page 37).

I hope you'll enjoy working up these patterns, and that they'll bring an extra dose of comfort to your life. Most importantly, I hope they each give you that smile yarn lovers get when we finish a project and love the end result so much that we say to ourselves, "I made that."

CHOOSING YOUR MATERIALS and ESSENTIAL TOOLS

What I love about these projects is that they don't require many tools to get started! All you need is some yarn and crochet hooks to begin.

Yarn Used

While some projects in the book can be worked up faster than others, you'll see everything can be quick and cute with the right yarn! I do love the awesome squishiness of a bulky or super bulky weight yarn, as well as the defined textures you can get with a worsted weight and DK yarn. I had a lot of fun designing everything in this book using my favorites. A lot of my garments are worked up using yarn with a wool content, since it has a great stitch memory and helps the garment keep its shape. Some of my favorite yarn lines are used in the book, but all should be easy to substitute if you're unable to get them locally. Matching up the company's gauge on the yarn labels is a great indication that the yarns have a similar thickness to help you achieve the gauge listed in each pattern.

Hooks Used

These patterns were designed using Clover Amour Hooks, and my largest hook is a Boye. These have been a favorite of mine for years. These hooks have a tapered tip, which I find doesn't drag on my yarn or split

it, helping me to keep a nice tension throughout my projects. If you need any size hook listed in the book, you can find all the links to them in my Amazon storefront (link on my website, whistleandwool.com). With that said, we all have a different grip and crocheting technique, so definitely find hooks that work best for you. The wrong hook can take a project from enjoyable to difficult instantly.

My largest hook, the Boye 15.75, is made from plastic and may take a swatch or two to get used to, but it is definitely worth it. Trust me, you'll love seeing the textures and projects you can make with it. It's light as a feather since it's a plastic hook, and once you get a few rows in, muscle memory will take over and have that cardigan flowing off your hook in no time!

Note: Keep in mind that you may need a different size hook than I used. Even if a pattern uses a 15.75 hook, your gauge may need the 15 mm to match. I recommend selecting your hook by first matching the mm stated in the pattern, as some companies will vary the letter used for US sizes per mm, whereas the mm is always accurate to sizing. See "Let's Swatch! Ten Minutes Will Save Your Fit" (page 12) for details.

LET'S SWATCH! TEN MINUTES *will* SAVE YOUR FIT

How does taking ten minutes to swatch save your new project? Let me tell you!

Everyone has their own tension and style of crochet, so a swatch is needed to make sure your stitch width and length are similar while using the same hook. For instance, I may use a 10 mm hook for a particular pattern, but to match my stitch width and row height, you may need an 8 mm. We don't all have the same tension, which means tightness or looseness will vary. If you've ever made a dishcloth that turned out the size of a placemat, or your dishcloth was so small that you now have a coaster, you either needed a smaller or bigger hook, or your yarn wasn't the right substitute.

The gauge stated in each pattern is a mini version of the finished project you're making, which helps you achieve the correct sizing!

Taking the time to swatch can feel like time wasted, when you could otherwise be knee-deep into your favorite new project. I totally get it. But taking those ten minutes to see if the hook and yarn you're using are correct could make the difference between that epic "Oh yeah, I made that!" moment when you finish your project and working for 6 hours on a blanket or cardigan that you can't even use or wear. I promise it's worth it.

A simple trick I like to use is to make the swatch feel like time well-spent: Imagine your swatch is something essential for the project. When we think our time isn't wasted, we feel good about it, like it's a necessary step in our project journey. If you imagine it's a pocket for the cardigan you're making and discover that pocket's tension is way off because of the hook and yarn you used, it will save you time in the long run. You'll be right where you need to be to make adjustments before wasting a day of stitching. Or, you'll love it and be excited to keep going. Now, you can happily get started on your project knowing it'll be great.

Have I convinced you to make a swatch? I hope so! Now let me help you make one!

To create a swatch and see whether or not you'll meet my gauge, first begin by seeing what the pattern says we need to match.

For example, a pattern's gauge might read as follows:

10 sts x 10 rows = 5″ (13 cm) of dc

This means that with the hook I used for the pattern, I got ten stitches in this 5-inch (13-cm) square.

The number of inches a swatch is taken over may vary per pattern due to the size of the yarn or stitch used, so the inches we're measuring across is important to keep in mind.

It's best to make your swatch slightly bigger than what the pattern states so that you can measure in the center of your square. Why? The edge stitches, as well as the top and bottom rows, vary in tension and tend to stretch, whereas your center is where your stitching pace and tension remain the most consistent. The middle will give you a more accurate reading.

So, for this example, you would add two additional stitches to each side as well as two additional rows along the top and bottom.

Begin with the recommended hook size used in the pattern, chain 14, plus a few more for a turning chain; for this example, let's chain 16. In the 3rd chain from the hook, dc14 for the row. This gives you two additional stitches on either side for the measurement. Next, we will crochet our rows. Crochet four more rows than stated, for a total of 14—ch2, turn, dc14.

> **Note:** If this is a larger project like a blanket or a garment, I recommend working a swatch double the size, and then measuring the center 5 inches (13 cm). This will help mimic the stretch the project will have for a more accurate measurement.

Using your ruler, measure along the center of the swatch to count how many stitches you get within the 5 inches (13 cm). Next, measure your ten center rows, not including the first and last couple of rows.

Did we match up? If so, now you can move into the pattern knowing your project will match mine.

What to Do if Your Gauge Is Off

A few factors can affect this. By adjusting the hook and yarn used, you can adjust your gauge so that we are identical.

How to adjust:

- If your swatch has fewer stitches than the number of stitches indicated, make a new swatch again using a smaller hook.
- If your swatch has more stitches, make a new swatch using a larger hook.

What if you can't match both numbers perfectly? For all the patterns in this book, I tried to design things that will help keep this easy to manage.

For an overall adjustment, I find it best to match your stitches per inch (2.5 cm) so that the width of the garment or blanket will come out properly and fit similarly to the modeled photos. Rows can be added to adjust for the garment length.

> **EXCEPTION TO THE RULE:** There's always one, right? A few of my designs/garments are worked side to side, such as the Coastal Cardigan (page 37). This means the chest measurement or blanket width is measured by the row gauge. The rows equal the width here. So, for this swatch, you'll want to focus more on your row gauge matching mine. To adjust the length, add more chains to the start of your project, which is highlighted in the Notes section of these patterns to help you along the way.

PATTERN READING TIPS
and TECHNIQUES

In this section, you will find simple explanations and photo tutorials for some of the terms and textures I use in the book. All patterns are written using US terminology.

Reading the Pattern

Prepare. Giving a pattern a quick read-through before you begin is a good way to prepare for what you will be doing and know what sections you'll be working through. This can also give you a chance to look up any techniques that may be new to you, giving you an opportunity to practice them before you begin.

Abbreviations are used to make reading the pattern quicker. Each abbreviation will be referenced in the Abbreviations section of each pattern.

RS/WS are used throughout a pattern to let you know what side of the project should be in front of you.

Parentheses are used throughout a pattern for multiple reasons. They help separate size directions and stitch counts, making it easier to follow along for your size. Mid-row, such as "(hdc1, ch1, hdc1) in the first st" lets you know these stitches are worked into the same stitch, for an increase or texture. Parentheses can also help denote that a particular order of stitches is worked as a repeat for the row. The example "(dc1, BPdc1), repeat for the row," means to dc1 in one stitch, BPdc1 in the next stitch, and continue in that order. Context will help determine what the parentheses are drawing your attention to.

Square brackets at the end of a row's instructions are used to show the stitch count at the end of the row or round. If an increase or decrease was made by adjusting the stitch count, you'll see the new counts like this: [6 sts]. This allows you to stop and count your stitches to make sure you are on track before moving on. There are times I'll reiterate a stitch count that hasn't changed if there are a lot of chains or texture, so that you can verify your stitch count is where it should be.

Asterisks are used in a pattern to let you know where a repeat begins and to repeat the instructions following it until otherwise stated. If it says "repeat after * for the row," the stitch instructions following the * will be worked all the way until your last stitch. If the row says, "repeat after * until the last 2 sts," keep repeating the stitches stated after the * until the last two stitches, and then work the remaining two stitches as instructed.

Sizes. Some patterns throughout the book will have multiple sizes listed. For example, if you see XS (S, M, L, XL) (2X, 3X, 4X, 5X), the instructions throughout the pattern and finished stitch counts at the end of every row will appear in the same order, so that you can keep track of the size you are making and any individual instructions there may be for your size. Underlining or highlighting ahead of time all the stitch counts for the size you're working on can make flowing through the pattern easier.

Counting Chains from the Hook

Starting chains are often used when beginning a new project and form the foundation on which you build the rest of the project. Once you make your chain, you'll work stitches into the chain. When instructed, "Starting in the 2nd chain or starting in the 3rd chain," this refers to the number of chains from the hook we will work into to begin the row. The chains skipped will become the row's beginning chain. The 1st chain is the one with the active loop on your hook.

Turning Chain

At the beginning of every row, we have a beginning chain to raise the height of the row. Sometimes this chain counts as a stitch towards the total row count, and sometimes it does not. This affects where your first stitch gets placed. If your turning chain doesn't count as a stitch, the first stitch in the row is worked into the stitch at the base of the chain, as indicated by the white arrow in the photo above. If your starting chain counts as a stitch, your first stitch is worked into the next space, shown by the black arrow in the photo. Each pattern in the book will indicate in the Notes if the turning chain does or does not count as a stitch.

Magic Circle

This creates the start of a circular project (a project crocheted in the round) that allows the center to cinch up tight, as your stitches are worked into an adjustable loop (Photos A and B). If you find working a magic circle difficult, depending on your preference or crochet level, you can choose an alternate method of a ch3, and work all your stitches into the first ch. This method does create a bigger circular gap than a magic circle, and can't be cinched tight.

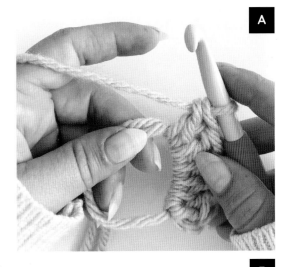

Switching Colors

For the patterns in this book, I switched colors on the new row, meaning I began my new rows' starting or turning chains with the new color. Another option would be to switch your color before the new row begins. To do this, just before you pull your last loop through of your row's last stitch, drop the yarn you are using and pull the new color through instead. Then continue onto your next row with your new color. Use whichever method you find more visually appealing.

work your stitches into the circle

pull to cinch
up the circle

Fch's ch1

begin the
Fch's here

Foundation Chain Half Double Crochet

A foundation chain is a method of working the starting chain and the first row at the same time. Working them at the same time avoids a turn after the initial starting chain. To create a foundation chain:

1. (Photo A) Yarn over and insert your hook into the base of the last stitch worked.

2. (Photo B) Pull up a loop. You should have three loops on your hook.

3. Yarn over and pull up a loop through the first loop (only) on the hook (referred to as your base chain stitch for the remaining half double crochet stitch row).

4. (Photo C) Yarn over and pull through all three loops on the hook. This completes your first half double crochet stitch.

5. To continue your row, yarn over and insert your hook into the base chain you created in Step 3.

6. Yarn over and pull up a loop to create your next base chain stitch.

7. Yarn over and pull through all three loops on your hook to complete your next half double crochet stitch.

8. Repeat after Step 3 until you've reached the number of stitches you need for the row.

Half Double Crochet 2 Together

You can use this method to create a decrease by crocheting two stitches together, which will remove one stitch from your row or round's stitch count. To do this, yarn over your hook and insert it into the next stitch, then pull through so you have three loops on your hook. Yarn over again, insert it into the next stitch, and pull through again so you have four loops on your hook. Yarn over again and pull through all four loops on your hook.

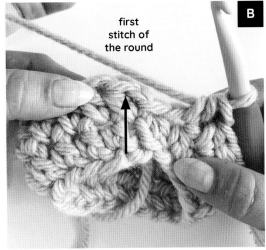

Continuous Rounds

Working in continuous rounds or a spiral means we will not transition to a new round by working a slip stitch and a chain when we reach the end. Continue crocheting around by working the beginning of the new round in the first stitch from the previous row (Photo A). This is a very easy way to work in the round, and you'll see a slight spiral tilt to your work as you keep going.

Work your round until you get back to the start of the round (Photo B). Instead of working a slip stitch into the top of the beginning chain, work your new stitch into it (Photo C). Continue working your rounds for the amount stated in the pattern. To keep track of rounds, you can place a marker in the first stitch you began your spiral with and keep replacing the marker in the new stitch that's worked into it (Photo D).

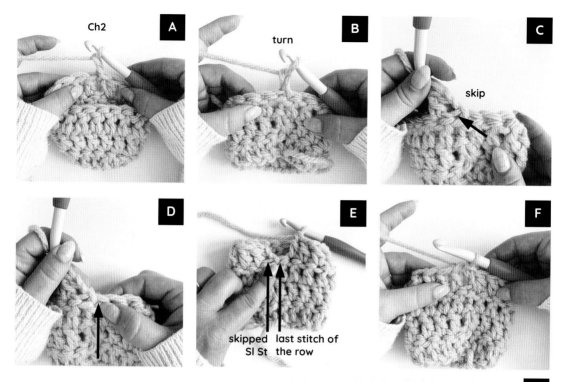

Joined Turning Rounds

This technique allows you to work in the round, while keeping the joined seam straight, such as on a sleeve. Begin the round with a ch2 (Photo A), turn (Photo B) and do **not** work into the slip stitch join from the previous round. It doesn't count as a stitch, so skip it (Photo C). Work your round. When you get to the end, your last stitch gets worked into the space at the base of the turning chain (Photo D). This helps keep the joined seam straight, as well, by keeping stitch placement consistent (Photo E). Slip stitch into the top of the turning chain to join in the round (Photos F and G).

previous rows Sl St join

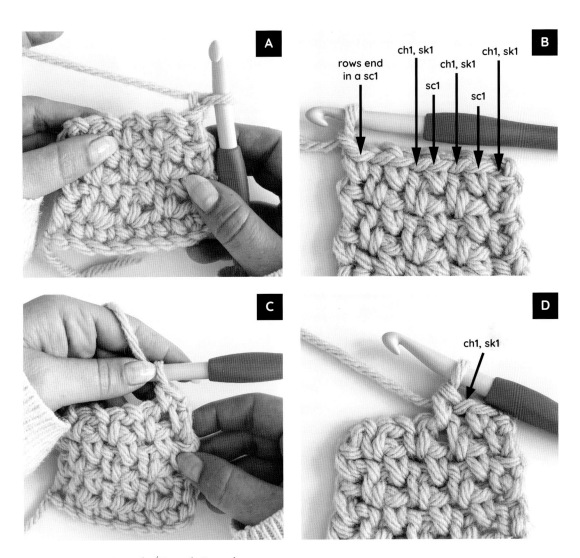

Linen Stitch/Seed Stitch

A linen stitch works up so quickly and gives a lovely texture. With a simple chain and single crochet, you can work up this "ch1, sk1, sc1" repeat (Photo A).

Continue to repeat this pattern of chaining 1, skipping a stitch and then single crocheting into the previous row's chain space until you reach the end of your row (Photo B). The single crochets always go into the previous row chain space (Photo C), and the chain 1s always go over the previous row's single crochet (Photo D). Every row will end in a single crochet.

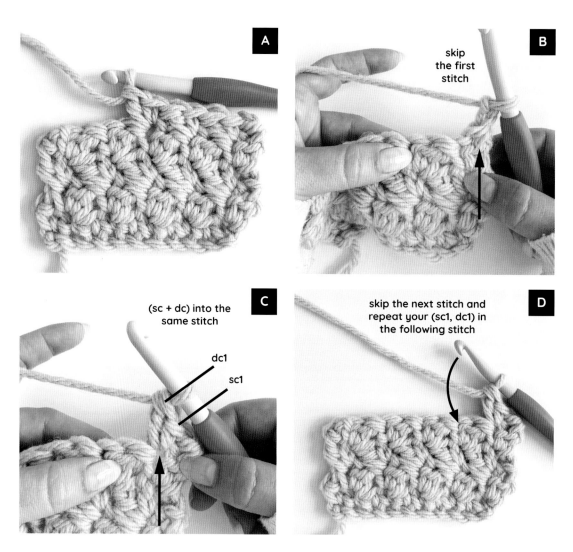

Suzette Stitch

This texture is worked up by skipping one stitch and placing two stitches in the following stitch (Photo A). Skip the first stitch (Photo B), work a single crochet and dc1 into the next stitch (Photo C). Continue with this pattern. By skipping a stitch and adding two in the next, the stitch count remains the same. Each set of (sc1, dc1) falls into the single crochet of the previous row (Photo D).

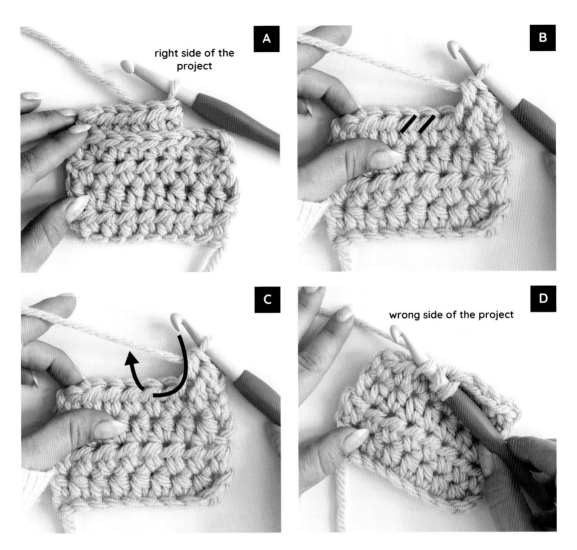

right side of the project

wrong side of the project

Half Double Crochet in the 3rd Loop

This stitch is worked on a Wrong Side row, so that the texture shows up on the Right Side (Photo A). Working into this stitch pushes the top "V" of the stitch to the front of the work. This stitch can be used to mimic a knit look. When you work this technique, you're inserting your hook into the diagonal bar located right under the standard "V" part of the stitch (Photos B and C). Yarn over like you would with a standard half double crochet; then insert your hook into the diagonal bar, and then complete the stitch like a standard half double crochet, as shown in Photo D (yarn over and pull the stitch through all the loops on your hook).

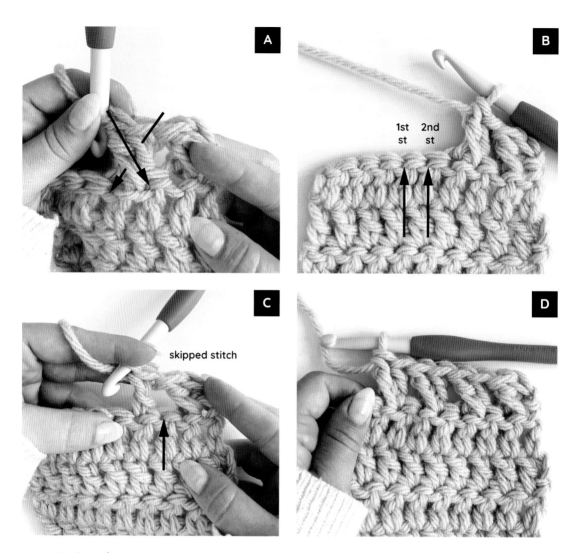

X Stitch

This stitch creates an "X" from crisscrossing the stitches (Photo A). This stitch is worked by skipping a stitch, working a double crochet and then working a double crochet into the next stitch. Then, working in front of the first stitch made, double crochet into that previously skipped stitch (Photo B). It's very easy to work, but as you do, just be sure to only work one stitch per stitch. As you work your next X stitch in the row, be sure to skip the first stitch (Photo C) so that your second double crochet doesn't go into the same space as your previous double crochet (Photo D).

Between the Stitch Posts

Working between the stitches is an easy way to get a woven-like texture (Photo A). Instead of placing the hook under the top "V" of the stitch, you work it underneath, between the posts of the stitches (Photo B).

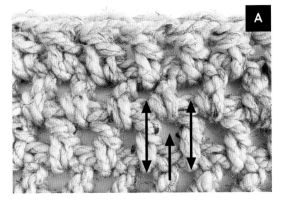

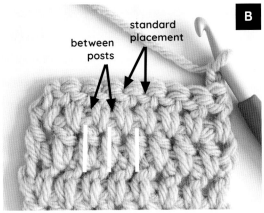

Slip Stitch Seam Method

Line up your edges to seam. Attach the yarn with a chain 1 at the bottom right-hand side edge. With the working yarn beneath the project, insert your hook top down into both loops of the next stitch, and then insert your hook top down into both loops of the parallel stitch on the left-hand side. Yarn over your hook with the yarn underneath and pull it through all four loops on the hook for a slip stitch seam.

Whip Stitch

I used this method throughout the book when sewing sleeves onto a cardigan or when sewing shoulder edges together. This is a beginner friendly method and makes seaming easy. To whip stitch, line up the two edges that will be sewn together. Before sewing, make sure the piece's orientation is properly lined up. Insert your yarn needle under both top loops of the stitch in front of you and the stitch directly across it. Pull the yarn all the way through to complete the stitch. Continue working until your section is seamed.

Fastening Off

When you've completed a section in the pattern, you will be instructed to fasten off and weave in your ends. Fastening off is what you do to close out a stitch, so your work doesn't come undone. Cut your yarn leaving a 5- to 6-inch (13- to 15-cm)-long tail. Using your hook, pull that loose end through the loop on your hook. Once the end of the yarn is out, pull on the tail to tighten it. Now your yarn won't unravel, as this locks in your last worked stitch.

Weaving in the Ends

I recommend leaving a tail 5 to 6 inches (13 to 15 cm) in length so that you have enough room to weave it in easily and trim the ends when done. When I join a new skein mid-project or row, I like to tie a bow or loose knot to keep the ends taut and maintain tension until I weave them in.

Using your yarn needle, weave in your ends on the wrong side of your project so that it doesn't show on the right side (the pretty side). To make sure the ends won't unravel after a lot of use or washing, weave along one direction and then turn to work in the other to really lock in the end.

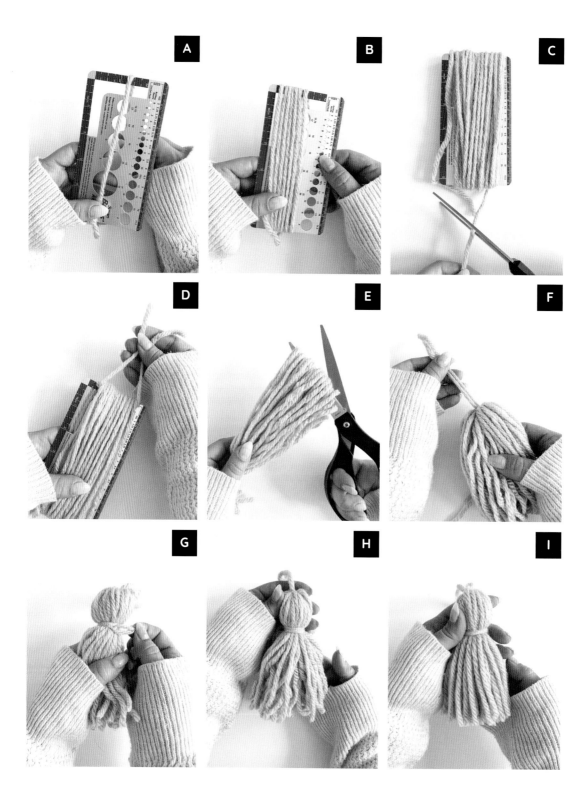

Tassels

Reference the photos on the left to complete these steps.

Tassels can add a cute finishing detail to so many projects. Throughout the book, I have a few projects that you could easily add tassels to for a fun customization, such as the Ridgeway Throw (page 85) and the Shelter Shawl (page 63). I thought it'd be neat to include this tutorial in case it comes in handy for you.

1. Cut a piece of cardboard to 5" (13 cm) in height, or use your gauge ruler (Photo A).

2. Wrap the yarn around your cardboard or ruler as many times as necessary to achieve your desired thickness. Cut your yarn (Photos B and C).

3. Cut a 7" (18-cm) length of yarn and loop it under the yarn along the top and tie it into a knot to secure the yarn (Photo D).

4. Remove the yarn from your winder, and cut the opposite end's loops to make the fringe (Photo E).

5. Cut a 7" (18-cm) length of yarn and while holding the yarn together, wrap it around all the yarn about an inch down from the top. Knot and hide your end inside the tassel (Photos F and G).

6. Steam block your tassel (see Blocking for instructions, right) and trim the ends even (Photos H and I).

Blocking

Blocking is like the clear coat of a manicure. It adds that last bit of polish to make your project look fantastic! It opens up stitch textures, smooths edges and can help define an item's shape and sizing. I used steam blocking for everything in this book; I find it easy and convenient. To steam block your own projects, you'll need a steamer and a set of blocking mats. Place your project on your blocking mats and hover your steamer about an inch or two above the project and keep it continually moving, much like you would a blow dryer. You don't want to overheat a section. If an edge or section of the project is curling, you can use blocking pins to keep it flat on your blocking mats while it cools. You can also use blocking as a means of gently stretching a garment to a final sizing if you're just a smidge off. You can find all of these supplies in my Amazon storefront (link on my website, whistleandwool.com).

Project Aftercare

When caring for your finished projects, I recommend referring to the yarn label's instructions. For instance, Wool Ease Thick and Quick allows for a gentle machine wash and dry. If using this method, be careful not to stretch the garment when moving it from the washer to the dryer. If a yarn requires hand washing and air drying, I again use my blocking mats to lie the project flat and take care to not stretch the wet garment or bag because this can permanently alter the measurements. When storing my finished items, I fold and leave them on shelves, as I do for my yarn, until my next use.

QUICK *but* COMFY CARDIGANS

A cardigan you can make in under a day? Yep! I had so much fun designing these cute pieces for that instant gratification! You can pair these with all of your outfits, and no one will believe you made them in a day. From bulky to super bulky, the Sway Sweater (page 55) to the Coastal Cardigan (page 37), all of these garments have an awesome, oversized comfiness and are full of pretty textures!

DUNE VEST

Skill Level: Basic • Project Time: 4-8 hours

With its subtle knit look and oversized comfort, this vest will be the layering piece you keep coming back to. This vest is also worked from side to side, with no shoulder seams, which adds to its relaxed drape across the shoulders. This works up using a classic hdc but working into the third loop, which pushes the V part of the stitch forward, creating this knit look—it's that EASY!

Sizes

- XS/S (M/L, XL/2X, 3X/5X)

Materials

Yarn

- Lion Brand Yarn, Super Bulky Weight, Wool Ease Thick and Quick (80% Acrylic, 20% Wool), 87 yd (80 m), 5 oz (140 g)

Shown In

- Driftwood

Yardage/Meterage

- 478 (565, 674, 761) yd [437 (517, 616, 696) m]

Hooks

- US Q (15.75 mm)
- US P (12 mm)

Notions

- Yarn needle
- Scissors

Gauge

- US Q (15.75 mm) hook or size needed to obtain gauge
- 8 sts x 6 rows = 6" (15 cm) in hdc (blocked)

Finished Measurements

- **For reference:** Model is 5'3" (160 cm) wearing a M/L
- **Based on chest measurements:** 30/34 (38/42, 46/50, 54/62)" [76/86 (96.5/107, 117/127, 137/157.5) cm]
- **Fit is oversized:** 8–16" (20–40.5 cm) positive ease included
- **Finished Chest (A):** 44 (52, 62, 70)" [112 (132, 157.5, 178) cm]
- **Armhole Depth (B):** 7 (8, 9, 10)" [18 (20, 23, 25.5) cm]
- **Shoulders to Bottom Hem (C):** 29" (73.5 cm)

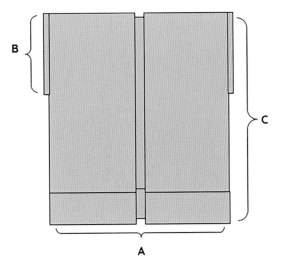

Abbreviations

BPdc	back post double crochet
ch	chain
dc	double crochet
FPdc	front post double crochet
FHDC	foundation chain half double crochet
hdc	half double crochet
RS	right side
st(s)	stitch(es)
Sl St	slip stitch
WS	wrong side

Notes

1. Beginning chain at the start of the row does not count as a stitch in this pattern.

2. When joining in the round, Sl St into the top of the beginning chain.

3. The loose gauge/tension will add an airy lightness to this design, while the wool content of the yarn will help it keep its shape.

4. This pattern uses an FHDC. If you aren't familiar with this stitch, I recommend doing a strand of them separately, like a gauge swatch, to get the muscle memory. This stitch is used instead of a beginning chain on the Second Panel because it keeps the textures on the right side.

5. The vest is constructed in one large piece worked from side to side, and then folded down at the shoulders, lengthwise. Side seams are then sewn up to create the vest shape.

6. Use a whip stitch (page 25) for sewing up the seams.

7. This vest is worked side to side, so your rows determine the chest measurement. The stitches worked determine your length.

8. The cardigan may appear short compared to the photo until you add the bottom hem. The hem adds weight to the sts, which increases the length, as well as the additional rows added.

9. If you need to add/remove length to adjust for height and preference, follow the formula below.

10. The piece is folded in half at the finishing stage, so four additional chains at the beginning equals 1.5" (4 cm) in additional length. The number of starting chains should always be even since it's halved at the end. To remove length, start with fewer chains. If you adjust your starting chain when you get to the back section, you won't work the number stated; you would divide your starting sts in half, and only work that amount.

How the Vest Works Up

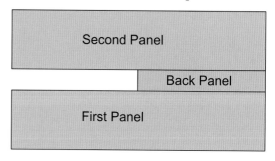

Dune Vest Pattern

First Panel Using the larger hook, Ch66 (loosely).

Row 1: (RS) Starting in the 3rd ch from the hook, hdc64. [64 sts]

Row 2: (WS) Ch2, turn, hdc in the 3rd loop (below the front loop) for the row.

Row 3: Ch2, turn, hdc for the row.

Rows 4-10 (12, 14, 16): Repeat Rows 2 and 3, ending on a Row 2 repeat.

Back Panel

Row 1: (RS) Ch2, turn, hdc32. [32 sts]

Row 2: (WS) Ch2, turn, hdc in the 3rd loop for the row.

For XL/2X, 3X/5X sizes only, work these additional two rows:

Rows 3-4: Repeat Rows 1 and 2.

Second Panel *For all sizes:*

Row 1: (RS) Ch2, turn, hdc32, without turning, FHDC 32 sts to increase the st count to match the stitch count of the First Front Panel. [64 sts]

> **Note:** As you work your FHDCs, make sure to have the ch step loose so that the panel doesn't pull tight and appear shorter than your First Front Panel.

Row 2: (WS) Ch2, turn, hdc in the 3rd loop (below the front loop) for the row.

Row 3: Ch2, turn, hdc for the row.

Rows 4-10 (12, 14, 16): Repeat Rows 2 and 3, ending on a Row 2 repeat.

> **Note:** The First and Second Panels should have the same number of rows.

Fasten off and weave in the ends.

Finishing

Lay the piece flat, RS up.

Fold the First and Second Panels in half lengthwise to create your cardigan's shape. The top fold will now be the shoulders. The RS of the panels now face each other.

Side Seams

Starting at the bottom hem and using a piece of yarn twice the length of the seam, sew up the sides of the vest, stopping 7 (8, 9, 10)" [18 (20, 23, 25.5) cm] from the shoulders for the sleeve opening.

Weave in the ends.

Bottom Hem

Using the smaller hook, turn the vest RS out to attach your yarn at the bottom hem with a ch2.

Row 1: (RS) Dc along the hem edge.

> **Note:** Ensure your dcs are evenly spaced along the bottom edge so that it lays flat. If it buckles, you have too many sts; if it pulls tight, you have too few. I alternated working a dc1 along a row ending, followed by dc2 in the next. Work according to your gauge. It is not important whether you finish with an even or odd number of stitches.

Row 2: Ch2, turn, (dc1, BPdc1) repeat for the row.

> **Note:** If you started with an odd number of sts, you will end on a dc1.

Row 3: Ch2, turn, dc1 the dc stitches, FPdc1 the post stitches for the row.

Row 4: Ch2, turn, dc1 the dc stitches, BPdc1 the post stitches for the row.

Row 5: Repeat Row 3.

> **Note:** After Row 5, ch2, and with the RS still facing, turn to work up the lapel, instead of the hem.

Lapel and Bottom Edging

Row 1: (RS) Using the smaller hook, dc up the row ends of the hem and then work into the worked sts on the lapel, across the row ends for the neckline, and then back down the lapel sts. The stitch count is flexible here; just make sure each side has the same amount of sts, and the hem is not pulling or stretching the vest length.

Next: Once you complete the row, pivot your hook to begin working along the bottom hem; ch2, Sl St into each st along the bottom hem for a clean edge. Sl St to join in the round when you get back to the other lapel edge.

Fasten off and weave in the ends.

Sleeve Edging

(RS) Use the larger hook. In the center of the underarm, attach your yarn with a ch1, hdc around the sleeve opening and Sl St to join in the round.

Repeat for both Sleeves.

Fasten off and weave in the ends.

Voila! You're done! Block your project (see page 27 for more instructions).

COASTAL CARDIGAN

Skill Level: Easy • Project Time: 4.5–7 hours (XS-XL),
8–12 hours (2X-5X)

Wool Ease Thick and Quick and a big hook allow you to create a wonderful, airy piece with lots of flowy drape, while the wool content of the yarn will help it keep its shape. It works up quickly and makes an amazing gift! One of my favorite designs from years back in my shop uses this yarn and hook combo, so I knew I had to create another garment with it for this book. It has the added fun details of pockets and a collar, and the fact that it's washable and dryable is a huge bonus, too!

Sizes

- XS (S, M, L, XL) (2X, 3X, 4X/5X)

Materials

Yarn

- Lion Brand Yarn, Super Bulky Weight, Wool Ease Thick and Quick (80% Acrylic, 20% Wool), 106 yd (97 m), 6 oz (170 g)

Shown In

- Navy

Yardage/Meterage

- 285 (298, 318, 330, 349) (367, 383, 399) yd [261 (272, 291, 302, 319) (335, 351, 365) m]

Hooks

- US Q (15.75 mm)
- US P (12 mm)

Notions

- Locking stitch markers or pins to attach the Collar
- Yarn needle
- Scissors

Gauge

- US Q (15.75 mm) hook or size needed to obtain gauge
- 5 sts x 4 rows = 4" (10 cm) in hdc (blocked)

Finished Measurements

- **For reference:** Model is 5'3" (160 cm), wearing a M
- **Based on chest measurement of:** 30 (34, 38, 42, 46) (50, 54, 58/62)" [76 (86, 96.5, 107, 117) (127, 137, 147/158) cm]
- **Fit is oversized.** 11–17" (28-43 cm) positive ease included
- **Finished Chest (A):** 45 (49, 53, 57, 61) (65, 69, 73)" [114.5 (124.5, 135, 145, 155) (165, 175, 185.5) cm]
- **Armhole Depth (B):** 6.5 (6.5, 7, 7, 8) (9, 9.5, 10.5)" [16.5 (16.5, 18, 18, 20) (23, 24, 26.5) cm]
- **Sleeves (C):** 16 (16, 14, 14, 12) (12, 10, 10)" [40.5 (40.5, 35.5, 35.5, 30.5) (30.5, 25.5, 25.5) cm]
- **Shoulders to Bottom Hem (D):** 27" (68.5 cm)

Abbreviations

BPdc	back post double crochet
ch	chain
dc	double crochet
FPdc	front post double crochet
hdc	half double crochet
RS	right side
sc	single crochet
scblo	single crochet into the back loop only
Sl St	slip stitch
st(s)	stitch(es)
WS	wrong side

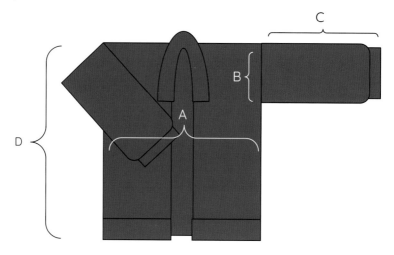

Notes

1. Beginning chain at the start of the row does not count as a stitch in this pattern, except on the collar section.

2. When joining in the round, Sl St into the top of the beginning chain.

3. The loose gauge/tension will add an airy lightness to this design, while the wool content of the yarn will help it keep its shape.

4. The cardigan is constructed in one large piece worked from side to side, and then folded lengthwise down at the shoulders. Side seams are then sewn up to create the cardigan's shape. Sleeves, the bottom hem, lapels and pockets are then added on.

5. Use a whip stitch (page 25) for sewing up the seams.

6. This cardigan is worked side to side, so your rows determine the chest measurement. The stitches worked determine your length.

7. The cardigan may appear short compared to the photo until you add the bottom hem. The hem adds weight to the sts, which increases the length, as well as the additional rows added.

8. The sleeves drop farther down the arm due to the chest circumference and oversized ease of the garment with a drop shoulder. Row count goes down as the sizes go up.

9. Your beginning st count affects your length. If more length is desired, this will be your formula to adjust the pattern:

   The piece is folded in half at the finishing stage, so four additional chains at the beginning equals 2.5" (6 cm) in total length. If you need an extra 3" (7.5 cm), add 6 sts. The number of starting chains should always be even, since it's halved at the end. To remove length, start with fewer chains. If you adjust your starting chain, when you get to the back section, you won't work the sts stated. You would divide your starting sts in half and only work that amount.

Coastal Cardigan Pattern

First Panel   Use the larger hook. Ch59 (loosely).

Row 1: Starting in the 2nd ch from the hook, hdc58. [58 sts]

Rows 2-9 (10, 11, 12, 13) (14, 15, 16): Ch1, turn, hdc for the row.

Do not cut the yarn; continue to the Back Panel.

Back Panel   *All sizes: We will now work half the stitches to create the back and neckline section.*

Row 1: Ch1, turn, hdc29. [29 sts]

> **Note:** If you started with a different number of stitches, you would now work half your stitches for this row.

Row 2: Ch1, turn, hdc for the row.

Row 3: Ch1, turn, hdc29, ch30 (loosely, or go up a hook size).

> **Note:** In Row 3, the ch30 increases the st count back to 58 sts (plus 1 for a turning ch) to begin working the Second Panel. If you started with a different beginning st count, ch as many as needed to match your First Panel's st count. Do not cut the yarn. Continue to the Second Panel.

Second Panel

Row 1: Being careful not to twist your ch and starting in the 2nd ch from hook, hdc58. [58 sts]

Rows 2-9 (10, 11, 12, 13) (14, 15, 16): Ch1, turn, hdc for the row.

> **Note:** The First and Second Panels should have the same number of rows.

Fasten off and weave in the ends.

Finishing

Lay the piece flat, RS up.

Fold the First and Second Panels in half lengthwise to create your cardigan shape. The top fold will now be the shoulders. The RS of the Panels now face each other.

Side Seams

Starting at the bottom hem and using a piece of yarn 20" (51 cm) long, sew up the side until 8 (8, 9, 9, 10) (11, 12, 13) sts from the shoulder. A total of 16 (16, 18, 18, 20) (22, 24, 26) sts (front and back) for the sleeve opening should be left.

Weave in the ends.

Bottom Hem

Use the smaller hook. With the RS facing you, attach your yarn with a ch2 at the bottom corner to begin working the hem (left-hand side if worn).

Row 1: (RS) Work dcs along the entire hem of the garment into the row endings of the First and Second Panels.

> **Note:** Ensure your dcs are evenly spaced along the bottom. If it buckles, you have too many sts; if it pulls tight, you have too few. I alternated working a dc1 along a row ending, followed by a dc2 along the next. Work according to your gauge. It is not important whether you finish with an even or odd number of stitches.

Row 2: Ch2, turn, (dc1, BPdc1) repeat for the row.

> **Note:** If you started with an odd number of sts, you will end on a dc1.

Row 3: Ch2, turn, dc1 the dc stitches, FPdc1 the post stitches for the row.

Row 4: Ch2, turn, dc1 the dc stitches, BPdc1 the post stitches for the row.

> **Note:** The hem measures 4" (10 cm); for additional length you can repeat rows 3 and 4, ending on a WS row before continuing on.

Fasten off and weave in the ends.

Lapel Use the smaller hook. With the RS facing you, attach the yarn with ch2 at the bottom corner of the First Panel (right-hand side if worn).

Row 1: (RS) Dc up the row ends of the hem and then work into the worked sts on the lapel, across the row ends for the neckline and then back down the lapel sts. The stitch count is flexible here; just make sure each side has the same amount of sts, and the hem is not pulling or stretching the cardigan's length.

Row 2: Ch2, turn, dc for the row.

Row 3: Ch2, turn, dc for the row.

Next: Once you complete the row, pivot your hook to begin working along the bottom hem, ch2. Sl St into each st along the bottom hem for a clean edge. Sl St to join in the round when you get back to the other lapel edge.

Sleeves *Repeat for both*

Round 1: (RS) Use the larger hook. In the center of the underarm, attach your yarn with a ch1, hdc around the sleeve opening, and Sl St to join in the round. [16 (16, 18, 18, 20) (22, 24, 26) sts]

> **Note:** It is not important whether your panels ended on RS or WS. You can still start your sleeve on the RS, and the texture will match.

Rounds 2–12 (12, 10, 10, 8) (8, 6, 6): Ch1, turn, hdc for the round; Sl St to join in the round.

> **Note:** The Cuff will add 4" (10 cm). Add or remove any length now to accommodate for height and preference. The last round worked is a WS round. Every round adds approximately 1" (2.5 cm).

Cuffs *Repeat for both*

Round 1: (RS) Using the smaller hook, ch2 (do not turn), dc for the round. Sl St to join in the round.

Rounds 2–4: Ch2, (FPdc1, dc1) repeat for the round. Sl St to join in the round.

Round 5: Ch1, Sl St for the round, and Sl St to join in the round.

Fasten off and weave in the ends. Use your yarn tail to cinch up any underarm gaps that remain.

Pockets _Make two_

Using the larger hook, ch10.

Row 1: Starting in the 2nd ch from the hook, hdc9. [9 sts]

Row 2-7: Ch1, turn, hdc for the row.

Edging: Ch1 (counts as a st), turn to work along the row ends. Sc1 in each row end along the edge. [8 sts]

Fasten off, leaving a tail three times the length of the pocket edge to sew the pocket onto the body.

Sewing on the Pockets Use a simple weaving stitch or your stitch preference. I sewed mine with the row texture going vertically to match the cardigan, along the bottom corner where the inside Bottom Hem and Lapel meet.

Weave in the ends.

Collar _Ch counts as a stitch for this section._

Using the smaller hook, ch7.

Row 1: Starting in the 2nd ch from the hook, sc6. [7 sts]

Rows 2-54: Ch1, turn, sc6blo.

Try this on around your neck to see if you'd prefer it longer or shorter.

Fasten off, leaving a tail twice the length of the Collar.

Pin the Collar, centered along the neckline. I didn't stretch mine. I just let it lay as is and pin it in place.

Sew it to the cardigan.

Weave in the ends.

Voila! You're done! Block your project (see page 27 for more instructions).

EMBRACE CARDIGAN

Skill Level: Easy • Project Time: 4.5-6 hours (XS-XL), 7-10 hours (2X-5X)

With this cardigan, you'll be buttoned up and embracing whatever new outing the day holds for you! Worked up in a bulky yarn, this three-quarter cuffed sleeve cardigan is full of texture and fun details. This design uses a simple technique to incorporate buttons so that you can wear it open or closed, and once you see how easy it is to make the button band, you'll be wanting to add buttons to all your cardigans.

Sizing

- XS (S, M, L, XL) (2X, 3X, 4X, 5X)

Materials

Yarn

- Lion Brand Yarn, Bulky Weight, Hue + Me (80% Acrylic, 20% Wool), 137 yd (125 m), 4.4 oz (125 g)

Shown in

- Desert

Yardage/Meterage

- 781 (834, 959, 1015, 1135) (1194, 1321, 1382, 1420) yd [714 (763, 877, 928, 1038) (1092, 1208, 1264, 1300) m]

Hook

- US M (9 mm)

Notions

- Locking stitch markers
- Yarn needle
- Scissors
- 5 buttons, 1 inch (27 mm)
- Sewing needle and thread for your buttons

Gauge

- 11 sts x 8 rows = 5″ (12.5 cm) in pattern (Rows 2 and 3 of the Back Panel repeated) (blocked)

Finished Measurements

- **For reference:** Model is 5'3" (160 cm) wearing a M
- **Based on chest measurement of:** 30 (34, 38, 42, 46) (50, 54, 58, 62)" [76 (86, 96.5, 107, 117) (127, 137, 147, 158) cm]
- **Fit is oversized.** 15" (38 cm) positive ease included
- **Finished Chest (A):** 45.5 (49, 53, 56.5, 60) (66.5, 70, 73.5, 77.5)" [115.5 (124.5, 135, 143.5, 152.5) (169, 178, 186.5, 197) cm]
- **Sleeves (B):** 11 (11, 10, 10, 9) (9, 8, 8, 6.5)" [28 (28, 25.5, 25.5, 23) (23, 20, 20, 16.5)]
- **Armhole Depth (C):** 7 (7, 8, 8, 9) (9, 10, 10, 11)" [18 (18, 20, 20, 23) (23, 25.5, 25.5, 28) cm]
- **Underarm to Bottom Hem (D):** 14.5" (37 cm)
- **Neck Opening (E):** 6" (15 cm)

Abbreviations

ch	chain
ch-sp	chain space
dc	double crochet
2dc	double crochet twice into the same stitch
dec	decrease
RS	right side
sc	single crochet
sk	skip
Sl St	slip stitch
WS	wrong side

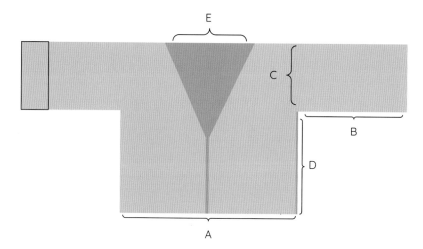

Notes

1. The starting chain is also referred to as the foundation chain in the pattern.

2. Beginning chain doesn't count as a stitch in this pattern unless otherwise stated.

3. This cardigan is constructed in panels that are sewn up to create the cardigan shape. Sleeves are then added on, along with the button band.

4. Use a whip stitch (page 25) for sewing up the seams.

5. When joining in the round, Sl St into the top of the beginning chain.

6. The sleeves drop farther down the arm due to the chest circumference and oversized ease of the garment with a drop shoulder. Row count goes down as the sizes go up.

Embrace Cardigan Pattern

Back Panel Ch52 (56, 60, 64, 68) (74, 78, 82, 86).

Row 1: (RS) Starting in the 3rd ch from the hook, dc for the row. [50 (54, 58, 64, 68) (72, 76, 80, 84) sts]

Row 2: (WS) Ch1, turn, *ch1, sk1, sc1, repeat after * for the row.

Row 3: Ch2, turn, *sk1, 2dc, repeat after * for the row.

Notes: For your repeats, your stitches fall in the same places. Your last stitch of your Row 2 repeat will always fall in the 2nd dc of the previous row.

For Row 3, your 2dcs will always fall in the ch-sp you made during Row 2.

Row 4: Ch1, turn, *ch1, sk1, sc1, repeat after * for the row.

Rows 5-34 (34, 36, 36, 38) (38, 40, 40, 42): Repeat Rows 3 and 4.

Note: Adjust length as needed for height or preference, ending on a WS row.

Fasten off and weave in the ends.

Front Left Panel *(when worn)*

Ch26 (28, 30, 32, 34) (38, 40, 42, 44).

Row 1: (RS) Starting in the 3rd ch from the hook, dc for the row. [24 (26, 28, 30, 32) (36, 38, 40, 42) sts]

Row 2: (WS) Ch1, turn, *ch1, sk1, sc1, repeat after * for the row.

Row 3: Ch2, turn, *sk1, 2dc, repeat after * for the row.

Row 4: Ch1, turn, *ch1, sk1, sc1, repeat after * for the row.

Rows 5–20: Repeat Rows 3 and 4.

> **Note:** If you added additional rows for length to your Back Panel, add the same number of extra rows now before continuing to the V-Neck Shaping.

V-Neck Shaping

Row 1: (RS) Ch2, turn, *sk1, 2dc, repeat after * until the last 4 sts, dc1 in each ch-sp from previous row for a decrease (2 sts worked), skipping the scs from the previous row. [22 (24, 26, 28, 30) (34, 36, 38, 40) sts]

Row 2: (WS) Ch1, turn, *ch1, sk1, sc1, repeat after * for the row.

Rows 3–8: Repeat Rows 1 and 2. [16 (18, 20, 22, 24) (28, 30, 32, 34) sts]

Rows 9–14 (14, 16, 16, 18) (18, 20, 20, 22): Repeat Rows 3 and 4 from the Front Left Panel, continuing in established pattern without decreases.

Fasten off and weave in the ends.

Front Right Panel *(when worn)*

Ch26 (28, 30, 32, 34) (38, 40, 42, 44).

Row 1: (RS) Starting in the 3rd ch from the hook, dc for the row. [24 (26, 28, 30, 32) (36, 38, 40, 42) sts]

Row 2: (WS) Ch1, turn, *ch1, sk1, sc1, repeat after * for the row.

Row 3: Ch2, turn, *sk1, 2dc, repeat after * for the row.

Row 4: Ch1, turn, *sk1, sc1, ch1, repeat after * for the row.

Rows 5–20: Repeat Rows 3 and 4.

> **Note:** Ensure both panels have the same number of rows up to this point before continuing to the V-Neck shaping.

V-Neck Shaping

Row 1: (RS) Ch2 (counts as a st for this row), turn, sk2, dc1, *sk1, 2dc, repeat after * for the row. [22 (24, 26, 28, 30) (34, 36, 38, 40) sts]

Row 2: (WS) Ch1, turn, *ch1, sk1, sc1, repeat after * for the row.

> **Note:** Last st goes in the top of your turning ch from Row 1.

Rows 3-8: Repeat Rows 1 and 2. [16 (18, 20, 22, 24) (28, 30, 32, 34) sts]

Rows 9-14 (14, 16, 16, 18) (18, 20, 20, 22): Repeat Rows 3 and 4 from the Front Right Panel, continuing in established pattern without decreases.

Fasten off and weave in the ends.

Seaming

Shoulder Seams: Lay the Back Panel down, RS up. Lay the Front Panels on top of it with RS down and the outer edges aligned. RS should be facing each other, and the Front Panels should form the V-Neck in the center.

Using a piece of yarn twice the shoulder width, sew the shoulders together.

Side Seams: Using a piece of yarn twice the length of the side seam, sew the side seams leaving a 7 (7, 8, 8, 9) (9, 10, 10, 11)" [18 (18, 20, 20, 23) (23, 25.5, 25.5, 28) cm] gap from the shoulder seam.

Weave in the ends. Turn the garment right side out.

Button Band Placement

Row 1: With the garment RS up in front of you, attach the yarn with a ch1 at the bottom left corner (Right Panel if worn), sc1 per row ending up to the V-neck section, sc2 per Row 1 ending, sc1 per Row 2 ending, sc into each worked stitch around the collar, repeat stitch placement for the other side so each side has the same number of stitches.

> **Note:** Adjust as needed for the gauge. The lapel should lay flat; if it buckles, you have too many sts. If it pulls tight, you have too few.

Button Placement

This method will help you customize your cardigan (Photo A).

A

Notes: If you prefer no buttons, don't work the skipped chains for the button row; just work each stitch as you normally would.

Each locking stitch marker placed will be a buttonhole. The buttons in Photo A indicate where the buttons will be sewn after completing Row 3. If you'd prefer more or fewer buttons, you can place your preferred number of markers.

With the garment RS up in front of you, attach a locking stitch marker in the 2nd stitch up from the bottom hem/foundation chain on the left side (Right Panel if worn). This is where my button placement started. I evenly placed my remaining markers 4 sts apart (marker, st, st, st, st, marker), working up the lapel, with my last button placed at where the V-Neck started. Adjust this for your size and based on the amount of sts worked for Row 1 above. I used five buttons but using more or less buttons will be easy when you use this method for placement.

Row 2: (Button Row) (WS) Ch1, turn, sc until you reach your marker, *ch1, sk the stitch with the marker, sc to the next marker, repeat after * for the remaining row until the last st, sc1.

Row 3: (RS) Ch1, turn, sc for the row.

Note: Sc into the chains for the buttonholes (not around them) as you come to them.

Fasten off and weave in the ends.

Attaching Buttons Using a sewing needle and matching thread, with the garment RS up in front of you and the button holes on the left-hand side, line up the bottom hems. Sew your buttons on the right-hand side, along Row 2, so that they line up with the buttonholes on the other Button Band.

Sleeves *Make two*

Work around the sleeve opening.

Round 1: (RS) Attach yarn with a ch1 in the center of the underarm, sc30 (30, 36, 36, 40) (40, 44, 44, 46) around the sleeve opening, Sl St to join in the round. [30 (30, 36, 36, 40) (40, 44, 44, 46) sts]

Round 2: Ch2 (no turn), *sk1, 2dc, repeat after * for the round, Sl St to join in the round.

> **Note:** Worked in joined turning rounds for the remainder of the sleeve.

Round 3: (WS) Ch1, turn, *ch1, sk1, sc1, repeat after * for the round, Sl St to join in the round.

Round 4: Ch2, turn, *sk1, 2dc, repeat after * for the round; Sl St to join in the round.

Rounds 5–12 (12, 10, 10, 8) (8, 6, 6, 4): Repeat Rounds 3 and 4.

> **Note:** If additional sleeve length is needed due to height adjustments, adjust rows now before working your decreases. End on a RS round.

Sleeves decrease section

Round 13 (13, 11, 11, 9) (9, 7, 7, 5): Repeat Round 3.

Round 14 (14, 12, 12, 10) (10, 8, 8, 6): (Dec) (Photos B and C) Ch2, turn, sk2, *sk1, 2dc, repeat after * for the round, Sl St to join in the round. [28 (28, 34, 34, 38) (38, 42, 42, 44) sts]

Round 15 (15, 13, 13, 11) (11, 9, 9, 7): Repeat Round 3.

Round 16 (16, 14, 14, 12) (12, 10, 10, 8): (Dec) (Photo D) Ch2, turn, *sk1, 2dc, repeat after * for the round until the last 2 sts, sk2, Sl St to join in the round. [26 (26, 32, 32, 36) (36, 40, 40, 42) sts]

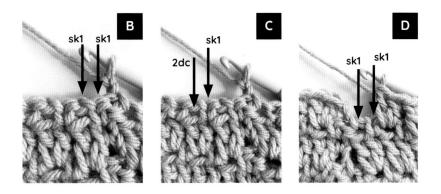

For XS-L sizes only, work the following rounds:

Round 17 (17, 15, 15, -) (-, -, -, -): Repeat Round 3.

Round 18 (18, 16, 16, -) (-, -, -, -): Repeat Round 4.

Round 19 (19, 17, 17, -) (-, -, -, -): Repeat Round 3.

Round 20 (20, 18, 18, -) (-, -, -, -): Ch2, turn, hdc for the round for a nice edging, Sl St to join in the round.

XL-5X sizes only, work the following rounds:

Round - (-, -, -, 13) (13, 11, 11, 9): Repeat Round 3.

Round - (-, -, -, 14) (14, 12, 12, 10): (Dec) Ch2, turn, sk2, *sk1, 2dc, repeat after * for the round, Sl St to join in the round. [- (-, -, -, 34) (34, 38, 38, 40) sts]

Round - (-, -, -, 15) (15, 13, 13, 11): Repeat Round 3.

Round - (-, -, -, 16) (16, 14, 14, 12): (Dec) Ch2, turn, *sk1, 2dc, repeat after * for the round until the last 2 sts, sk2, Sl St to join in the round. [- (-, -, -, 32) (32, 36, 36, 38) sts]

Round - (-, -, -, 17) (17, 15, 15, 13): Ch2, turn, hdc for the row for a nice edging, Sl St to join in the round.

All sizes

Fasten off and weave in the ends. Cuff your sleeve up for a cuff depth of approximately 1.5″ (4 cm), and tack it down with your yarn and sewing needle along the inside of the garment so that it stays cuffed when you wear it.

Voila! You're done! Block your project (see page 27 for more instructions).

SWAY SWEATER

Skill Level: Easy • Project Time: 5-6.5 hours (XS-XL), 7-9 hours (2X-5X)

The Suzette texture is one of my favorite crochet stitches I learned early on in my crochet journey. It adds an intricate look to this gorgeous, over-sized sweater, all while being super easy! This stitch creates a beautiful back-and-forth texture that almost appears to sway as the rows alternate between the stitch heights. A simple neck shaping finishes off this relaxing-to-work-up design so it's comfy but quick to do!

Sizes

- XS (S, M, L, XL) (2X, 3X, 4X, 5X)

Materials

Yarn

- Lion Brand Yarn, Bulky Weight, Hue + Me (80% Acrylic, 20% Wool), 137 yd (125 m), 4.4 oz (125 g)

Shown in

- Whisper

Yardage/Meterage

- 580 (613, 688, 703, 800) (815, 916, 930, 1030) yd [530 (561, 629, 643, 732) (745, 837, 851, 942) m]

Hook

- US M (9 mm)

Notions

- Yarn needle
- Scissors
- Locking stitch markers or pins

Gauge

- 8 sts x 7 rows = 4" (10 cm) in Suzette Stitch [sk1, (sc1, dc1) in the next stitch] (blocked)

Finished Measurements

- **For reference:** Model is 5'3" (160 cm) wearing a M
- **Based on chest measurement of:** 30 (34, 38, 42, 46) (50, 54, 58, 62)" [76 (86, 96.5, 107, 117), (127, 137, 147, 158) cm]
- **Fit is oversized.** 10" (25.5 cm) of positive ease included
- **Finished Chest (A):** 40 (44, 48, 52, 56) (60, 64, 68, 72)" [101.5 (112, 122, 132, 142) (152.5, 162.5, 172.5, 183) cm]
- **Sleeve Length (B):** 16 (16, 15, 13.5, 12.5) (11.5, 10.5, 9, 8)" [40.5 (40.5, 38, 34, 32) (29, 26.5, 23, 20.5) cm]
- **Armhole Depth (C):** 7 (7, 8, 8, 9) (9, 10, 10, 11)" [18 (18, 20.5, 20.5, 23) (23, 25.5, 25.5, 28) cm]
- **Underarm to Hem (D):** 8" (20 cm)
- **Neck Width (E):** 6 (6, 6, 6, 8) (8, 8, 8, 8)" [15 (15, 15, 15, 20) (20, 20, 20, 20) cm]

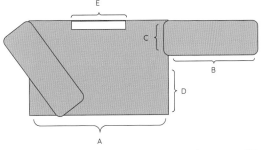

Notes

1. Beginning ch doesn't count as a stitch in this pattern.
2. This sweater body is constructed in panels that are sewn up to create the sweater shape. Sleeves are then made and sewn onto the body.
3. Garment Texture: When you see (sc1, dc1), these stitches are worked in the same stitch. Since we skip a stitch before it, your stitch count remains unchanged.
4. Use a whip stitch (page 25) for sewing up the seams.
5. The sleeves drop farther down the arm due to the chest circumference and oversized ease of the garment with a drop shoulder. Row count goes down as the sizes go up.

Abbreviations

ch	chain
dc	double crochet
dec	decrease
hdc	half double crochet
RS	right side
sc	single crochet
sk	skip
st(s)	stitch(es)
WS	wrong side

Sway Sweater Pattern

Back Panel Ch42 (46, 50, 54, 58) (62, 66, 70, 74).

Row 1: Starting in the 3rd ch from the hook, sc for the row. [40 (44, 48, 52, 56) (60, 64, 68, 72) sts]

Rows 2–26 (26, 28, 28, 30) (30, 32, 32, 34): Ch2, turn, *sk1, (sc1, dc1) in the next stitch, repeat after * for the row.

Note: Adjust length as needed for height or preference, ending on a WS row.

Fasten off.

Front Panel Ch42 (46, 50, 54, 58) (62, 66, 70, 74).

Row 1: (RS) Starting in the 3rd ch from the hook, sc for the row. [40 (44, 48, 52, 56) (60, 64, 68, 72) sts]

Row 2-24 (24, 26, 26, 28) (28, 30, 30, 32): Ch2, turn, *sk1, (sc1, dc1) in the next st, repeat after * for the row.

> **Note:** If you added/removed length to your Back Panel, add those additional rows now until the Front Panel is two rows shorter than the Back Panel. The last two rows are the Neck Shaping.

Neck Shaping *Shoulder One*

Row 25 (25, 27, 27, 29) (29, 31, 31, 33): Ch2, turn, *sk1, (sc1, dc1) in the next st, repeat after * for a total of 14 (16, 18, 20, 20) (22, 24, 26, 28) sts worked, leave the remaining sts unworked. [14 (16, 18, 20, 20) (22, 24, 26, 28) sts]

Row 26 (26, 28, 28, 30) (30, 32, 32, 34): Ch2, turn, *sk1, (sc1, dc1) in the next st, repeat after * for the row.

Fasten off.

Shoulder Two

Count 12 (12, 12, 12, 16) (16, 16, 16, 16) sts away from where you left off on Row 25 (25, 27, 27, 29) (29, 31, 31, 33), attach yarn with a ch2, *sk1, (sc1, dc1) in the next st, repeat after * for the remaining sts. [14 (16, 18, 20, 20) (22, 24, 26, 28) sts]

> **Note:** You should have 12 (12, 12, 12, 16) (16, 16, 16, 16) sts for neck opening.

Row 26 (26, 28, 30, 30) (32, 32, 32, 34): Ch2, turn, *sk1, (sc1, dc1) in the next st, repeat after * for the row.

Fasten off.

Shoulder Seaming

Lay the Back Panel down, RS up.

Lay the Front Panel on top of it so that the RSs are facing each other.

Using a piece of yarn twice the shoulder width, sew the Shoulders together from the outside edge, moving inward.

Weave in all the ends.

Sleeves Ch30 (30, 34, 34, 38) (38, 42, 42, 46).

Row 1: Starting in the 3rd ch from the hook, sc for the row. [28 (28, 32, 32, 36) (36, 40, 40, 44) sts]

Rows 2-26 (26, 24, 22, 20) (18, 16, 14, 12): Ch2, turn, *sk1, (sc1, dc1) in the next st, repeat after * for the row.

Note: Adjust sleeve length as needed for height and preferences. Add or remove rows as needed before continuing to the Cuff Decrease.

Cuff Decrease

Row 27 (27, 25, 23, 21) (19, 17, 15, 13): (RS) Ch2, turn, *sk1, hdc1, repeat after * for the row. [14 (14, 16, 16, 18) (18, 20, 20, 22) sts]

Row 28 (28, 26, 24, 22) (20, 18, 16, 14): (WS) Ch2, turn, hdc for the row.

Fasten off, leaving a tail that is twice the sleeve length for seaming.

Finishing

Attaching the Sleeves: Using pins or locking stitch markers, attach the Sleeves evenly to the sweater body, so that they are centered along the Shoulder seam and in place while you sew with the WS facing you.

Sew the sleeves to the body.

Side Seams: Fold the garment in half from the Shoulders, bringing the bottom hems together. The sweater should look inside out.

Using a piece of yarn twice the length of the side seam, sew up from the bottom hem to the Underarm. Repeat for both sides.

Sleeve Seams: Using your long tail, sew up the length of the Sleeve from the Cuff to the Underarm. Repeat for both sides.

Weave in all the ends.

Voila! You're done! Block your project (see page 27 for more instructions).

WRAPPED *in* WARMTH SHAWLS + WRAPS

If, like me, you love a layering piece that will ramp up any outfit and provide the perfect amount of coziness for when the weather is all over the place, then this is your section! From the Yesterday Wrap (page 69), with its lightweight to medium coverage, to the Shelter Shawl (page 63), which provides maximum warmth, all of these can be worked up in an afternoon at home and will be your favorites for years to come.

SHELTER SHAWL

Skill Level: Basic • Project Time: 5–5.5 hours

Sheltering from a storm and any cold breezes as the weather dips is easy peasy with this shawl! The bulky yarn adds warmth while the simple stitches help keep this layering piece flexible and easy to wrap you up in comfort! Shawls are some of my favorite things to create, and this pattern works up so quickly. You can mix and match any colorways to customize this for a gift or a lovely treat for yourself. This has enough length and width to drape around your shoulders or bundle around your neck, making this your soon-to-be favorite accessory.

Size
- One size

Materials

Yarn
- Lion Brand Yarn, Bulky Weight, Hue + Me (80% Acrylic, 20% Wool), 137 yd (125 m), 4.4 oz (125 g)

Shown in
- **Color A:** Whisper
- **Color B:** Magic Hour

Yardage/Meterage
- **Color A:** 411 yd (376 m)
- **Color B:** 153 yd (140 m)

Hook
- US M (9 mm)

Notions
- Stitch marker
- Yarn needle
- Scissors

Gauge
- 9 sts x 6 rows = 5" (12.5 cm) in dc (blocked)

Finished Measurements
- **Width (A):** 80" (203 cm)
- **Depth (B):** 27" (68.5 cm)

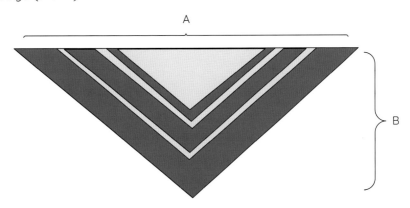

Abbreviations

ch	chain
ch-sp	chain space
dc	double crochet
Esc	extended single crochet
hdc	half double crochet
M	stitch marker
sc	single crochet
sk	skip
Sl St	slip stitch
st(s)	stitch(es)
RS	right side
WS	wrong side
X Stitch	See Techniques (page 24)

Notes

1. Beginning chain doesn't count as a stitch in this pattern, but all other chains count as a stitch for the row.

2. This shawl is worked from the top down.

3. Increases are worked on every row, at each end and the center. Six stitches are increased each row.

4. (Photo A) Throughout the pattern, I worked my stitches into the ch-sp's from previous rows but not into the ch itself.

5. I carried my yarn up between color changes. A sc border is added to the top edge of the shawl when you're done, which will cover up the carried yarn. If you prefer, you can cut your yarn between changes and weave in your ends after.

6. **Size Adjustments:** If you'd like to add width to your shawl, I recommend doing this in the first section of Color A since it's simple dc rows. The last row worked should be on the WS, so the remaining pattern stitch directions still line up. Please note that this will use more yarn and add weight to the overall finished item. To make your shawl smaller, just remove dc rows in Color A at the beginning and make sure your last row is worked on the WS.

Shelter Shawl Pattern

Body of the Shawl

With Color A, ch6.

Row 1: (RS) Starting in the 2nd ch from the hook, we will work our first increase (dc1, ch1, dc1), dc1 in the next ch, (hdc1, ch1, hdc1) in the next ch and place a M in the ch1 space to mark where your center increase will be, dc1 in the next ch, (dc1, ch1, dc1) in the last ch for your final increase. [11 sts, worked across 5 sts, 6 sts increased]

Rows 2-12: Ch3, turn, (dc1, ch1, dc1) in the first st, dc in each st until the M, remove M, (hdc1, ch1, hdc1) in the space and replace the M into the new ch1 st (See the Notes below), dc in each st until the last st, (dc1, ch1, dc1) in the last st. [77 sts, 6 sts increased each row]

> **Notes:** Your st count increases by 6 sts every row. For example, Row 3 [23 sts], Row 4 [29 sts], Row 5 [35 sts]. At the end of Row 12 your new count will be [77 sts]. (Photo B, page 67) When you get to your M, keep replacing the M back into the newly created ch1 in your (hdc1, ch1, hdc1) increase, so you don't lose your center increase position.

Row 13: (RS) With Color B, ch2, turn, (hdc1, ch1, hdc1) in the first st, Esc in each st until the M, remove M, (hdc1, ch1, hdc1) in the space and replace M, Esc in each st until the last st, (hdc1, ch1, hdc1) in last st. [83 sts]

Row 14: (WS) (Photo C, page 67) Ch3, turn, (dc1, ch1, dc1) in the first st, X Stitch until the M, remove M, (hdc1, ch1, hdc1) in the space and replace M, X Stitch until the last st, (dc1, ch1, dc1) in last st. [89 sts]

Rows 15-16: With Color A, repeat Rows 13 and 14. [101 sts]

Rows 17-20: With Color B, repeat Row 2. [125 sts]

Rows 21-22: With Color A, repeat Rows 13 and 14. [137 sts]

Rows 23-25: With Color B, repeat Row 2. [155 sts]

Row 26: Repeat Row 14. [161 sts]

Row 27: Repeat Row 2. [167 sts]

Row 28: Ch3, turn, (dc1, ch1, dc1) in the first st, (dc1, ch1, sk1) until the M (the st right before the M is a sk1), remove M, (hdc1, ch1, hdc1) in the space and replace M, (ch1, sk1, dc1) until the last st, (dc1, ch1, dc1) in last st. [173 sts]

Row 29: Ch3, turn, (dc1, ch1, dc1) in the first st, (dc1, ch1, sk1) until the st before the M, dc1, remove M, (hdc1, ch1, hdc1) in the space and replace M, dc1 in the next st, (ch1, sk1, dc1) until the last st, (dc1, ch1, dc1) in last st. [179 sts]

Row 30: Repeat Row 2. [185 sts]

Row 31: (RS) (Photo D) Ch2, turn, Sl St into every st for a finished edging (if your edging starts to pull in, Sl St looser or go up a hook size). [185 sts]

Fasten off Color A. With Color B, continue to Top Edging.

Top Edging

Step 1: With Color B, ch1, turn to begin to work along the top (straight edge) of the shawl. With the RS facing you, sc along the row endings until you reach the first Color A section worked (Rows 1–12), cut your yarn and attach Color A.

Step 2: (Photos E and F) Sc the edge until you reach the Color B section again, cut your yarn and attach Color B for the remainder.

> **Note:** I alternated between a sc2 and a sc1 along each row ending. Adjust as needed so this row lays flat. The shawl shouldn't buckle from too few stitches or ripple from too many.

Fasten off and weave in the ends.

Optional: Add tassels (see page 27 for more instructions) to the two ends and center point of your shawl with the remaining yarn.

Voila! You're done! Block your project (see page 27 for more instructions).

Rows 4-11: (Photo F) Ch3, turn, 2dc in the base of the turning ch, sk2, 3dc between the clusters in the previous row, *sk3, 3dc between the clusters in the previous row, repeat after * until the last 3 sts, sk2, 3dc in the last st. [33 sts]

Note: Stitch counts increase by 3 sts each row.

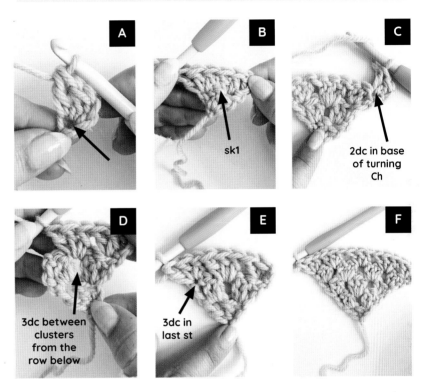

Row 12: Ch3, turn, sk2, 3dc between the clusters in the previous row, *sk3, 3dc between the clusters in the previous row, repeat after * until the last 3 sts, sk2, ch1, dc1 in the last st.

Row 13: Ch2, turn, 2dc in the space (between previous row's cluster and dc1), *sk3, 3dc between the clusters in the previous row, repeat after * until the last st, 3dc between the cluster and the ch3 turning ch from the row below.

Note: Work a turning ch2 on RS rows, ch3 on WS rows.

Row 14: Repeat Row 12.

Rows 15-40: Repeat Rows 13 and 14.

Rows 41–82: With Color B, repeat Rows 13 and 14.

> **Note:** If you prefer extra length for your wrap, you can add it now by ending on a WS row. Ensure that your row counts match for both pieces. More Color B yarn will be needed for additional length.

Fasten off and weave in the ends for your first panel. Work a second panel as above, but do not cut the yarn when you've completed your last row; we will begin there for seaming the two halves together.

Finishing and Seaming

(Photo G) Beginning with the live stitch from the panel you just completed, ch1, turn; you're now on the RS. Line up the two short ends of the shawl with wrong sides facing each other.

(Photos H and I) Sc the short ends together. Starting chains from the panels still count as a stitch. Work parallel stitches together so the edges line up perfectly.

Fasten off and weave in the ends.

Optional: I like the pop from a sc seam, adding to the texture of this wrap, but you can substitute this seam with your favorite method.

Voila! You're done! Block your project (see page 27 for more instructions).

IN a JIFFY SCARF

Skill Level: Basic • Project Time: 3-4 hours

With only 11 total rows to work, you'll fly through this stunning pattern. In just a few hours, you can add this stylish detail to your colder weather outfits. This gorgeous scarf is long enough to customize your wrap and has a ton of flexibility since it's worked up with a long triple crochet stitch, which is also wonderfully meditative and easy to memorize. Use a super soft, bulky yarn like I did, and you can make some incredible gifts for the ones you love.

Size
- One size

Materials

Yarn
- Lion Brand Yarn, Bulky Weight, Jiffy Bonus Bundle (100% Acrylic), 681 yd (623 m), 15.5 oz (410 g)

Shown in
- Cedar

Yardage/Meterage
- 378 yd (346 m)

Hook
- US M (9 mm)

Notions
- Scissors
- Yarn needle

Gauge
- 7 sts x 4 rows = 4" (10 cm) in pattern (RS: tc, WS: hdc) (blocked)

Finished Measurements
- **Length (A):** 97" (246.5 cm)
- **Width (B):** 11" (28 cm)

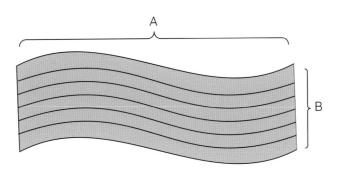

1. Beginning ch counts as a stitch in this pattern.

2. This scarf is worked lengthwise.

3. Ch loosely for your starting/foundation ch or go up a hook size for it. This helps to ensure your scarf isn't pulled tighter on one side.

4. To make your scarf longer, you can add more sts to your foundation chain.

5. **Gauge:** Work your gauge swatch over a repeat of Rows 2 and 3. If your turning chains seem tight on Row 3, try making a chain of 4 instead of 3.

Abbreviations

ch	chain
hdc	half double crochet
RS	right side
st(s)	stitch(es)
tc	triple crochet
WS	wrong side

In a Jiffy Scarf Pattern

Scarf Ch 172.

Row 1: (RS) Starting in the 4th chain from the hook, tc169. [170 sts]

Row 2: (WS) Ch2, turn, hdc for the row.

Row 3: Ch3, turn, tc for the row.

Rows 4–11: Repeat Rows 2 and 3.

Note: If you want to add more width to your scarf, continue in pattern, ending after a RS row.

Fasten off and weave in the ends.

Voila! You're done! Block your project (see page 27 for more instructions).

COZY *at* HOME

What's better than making handmade items for life's joyful moments at home? Make beautiful blankets for the kiddos to stay cozy under, like the Serene Throw (page 81), or snuggle up with a soft pair of Quick and Cozy Slippers (page 89) as you read your favorite book by the warm fire. In just a few hours or a long afternoon, you can add these pieces of modern luxury and handcrafted goodness to your home style!

SERENE THROW

Skill Level: Basic • Project Time: 6–8 hours

I love a slow start to the day as I sip my morning tea and bundle under a handmade cozy throw on the sofa as my pup sits next to me. The process of making this blanket will be as serene as the moments you'll experience when you're using it. The Serene Throw is worked up using one of my favorite (and easiest) stitches that adds a woven-like texture to your home décor. Dcs worked between the stitch posts add an airiness to this throw, keeping it flexible and squishy.

Sizes
- One size

Materials

Yarn
- Lion Brand Yarn, Super Bulky, Wool Ease Thick & Quick (82% Acrylic, 10% Wool, 8% Rayon), 106 yd (97 m), 6 oz (170 g)

Shown in
- Grey Marble

Yardage/Meterage
- 633 yd (579 m)

Hook
- US P/Q (15 mm)

Notions
- Yarn needle
- Scissors
- 4 faux fur poms, or materials below to make DIY poms

DIY Pom supplies (optional)
- A sharp tapestry needle (I use a leather needle so that my yarn fits through the eye, and it's sharp enough to go through the faux fur)

- Enough faux fur fabric to make 4, 6" (15 cm) squares
- A few handfuls of poly fill or any other material for filling the finished poms
- 4 sew-on snaps to have removable poms

Gauge
- 4.5 sts x 3.5 rows = 4" (10 cm) in dc between the st posts (blocked)

Finished Measurements
- **Length (A)**: 46" (117 cm)
- **Width (B):** 44.5" (113 cm)

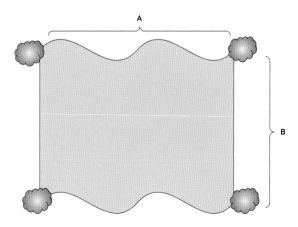

Notes

1. Beginning chain doesn't count as a stitch in this pattern.

2. For a wider throw, four additional chains at the beginning equals 3.5″ (9 cm) in additional width. Adjust as needed.

3. For a longer throw, four additional rows equal 4.5″ (11.5 cm) in additional length. Adjust as needed.

Abbreviations

ch   chain

dc   double crochet

st(s)   stitch(es)

Serene Throw Pattern

Throw Ch52.

Row 1: Starting in the 3rd ch from the hook, dc50. [50 sts]

Rows 2–40: Ch2, turn, dc50 between the st posts.

Note: Your last stitch is worked between the st post and the previous row's turning chain.

Fasten off and weave in the ends.

Voila! You're done! Block your project (see page 27 for more instructions).

Attaching the Pom Poms

Note: You can purchase four pre-made pom-poms from your local craft store or make your own DIY version using my tutorial.

Attach one pom-pom to each corner of the throw.

Using your matching yarn, you can sew the pom-poms to each corner for permanent placement and trim the ends when done.

For a removable method, you can use sew-on snaps. Sew one snap end to the blanket corner with matching yarn or thread, and then sew the other end of the snap onto the bottom of the pom-pom. Trim all ends. Now you can snap the pom-poms into place and unsnap them for a safe removal when washing the blanket.

DIY Pom Poms

Cut the fur fabric into 6″ (15 cm) squares.

You'll need a strong piece of yarn or thread doubled (I like to use Lion Brand Yarn 24/7 yarn); cut a piece long enough to work all the way around the square's edge.

(Photo A) WS facing you, work a running stitch all the way around the square.

(Photos B and C) Before we cinch it up, add a ping pong ball–sized amount of filling to the center. The semi-filled pom keeps them light, so they don't stretch and weigh down the corners of the throw.

(Photo D) Once filled, cinch it tight by pulling the yarn ends. Weave through the edges a few more times and knot the ends to make sure nothing will undo or loosen up. Do not trim the ends.

Photo E shows the size of the pom poms in reference to the blanket sts.

RIDGEWAY THROW

Skill Level: Easy • Project Time: 6–7.5 hours

Make this timeless modern throw with a minimalist luxury look in just one sitting! This pattern uses basic stitches, making it a relaxing project to work through. A post stitch worked strategically throughout the pattern makes this texture work up quickly before your eyes, allowing you to make this gorgeous throw in under eight hours! Drape it over a chair or wrap up in it as you enjoy a movie night.

Size

- One size

Materials

Yarn

- Lion Brand Yarn, Super Bulky Weight, Wool Ease Thick and Quick (80% Acrylic, 20% Wool), 106 yd (97 m), 6 oz (170 g)

Shown in

- Fisherman

Yardage/Meterage

- 942 yd (861 m)

Hook

- US P (12 mm)

Notions

- Yarn needle
- Scissors

Gauge

- 6 sts x 4 rows = 4" (10 cm) in dc (blocked)

Finished Measurements

- **Length (A):** 56" (142 cm)
- **Width (B):** 47" (119 cm)

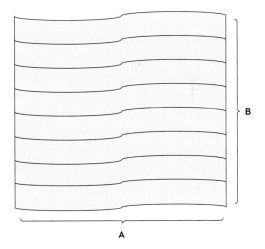

Abbreviations

ch	chain
dc	double crochet
FPdc	front post double crochet
RS	right side
sc	single crochet
st(s)	stitch(es)
WS	wrong side

Notes

1. Beginning ch counts as a stitch to give the throw the straight edges.

2. This pattern is worked lengthwise and from side to side to create vertical ridges.

3. Your beginning stitch count contributes to the throw's length, and the rows worked will equal the finished width.

Ridgeway Throw Pattern

Throw Ch85.

Row 1: (RS) Starting in the 3rd ch from the hook, dc83. [84 sts]

Rows 2–5: Ch2, turn, dc for the row. [84 sts]

Row 6: (WS) Ch2, turn, FPdc until the last stitch, dc1.

Rows 7–11: Ch2, turn, dc for the row.

Row 12: Ch2, turn, FPdc until the last stitch, dc1.

Rows 13–42: Repeat Rows 7—12.

Rows 43–46: Ch2, turn, dc for the row.

Row 47: (RS) Ch1, turn, sc for the row.

Fasten off and weave in the ends.

Voila! You're done! Block your project (see page 27 for more instructions).

QUICK *and* COZY SLIPPERS

Skill Level: Easy • Project Time: 1-1.5 hours for the pair

Invite a little added warmth into your life with this luxurious pair of quick and cozy slipper socks, and let your day at home begin in comfort. Make the set in under two hours using basic stitches, with a nice arched heel to help them fit your feet snug and not slip off. These will definitely add some cute to your cozy day!

Size
- Women's US 5/6 (7/8, 9/10, 11/12)

Materials

Yarn
- Lion Brand Yarn, Super Bulky Weight, Wool Ease Thick and Quick (82% Acrylic, 10% Wool, 8% Raylon), 106 yd (97 m), 6 oz (170 g)

Shown in
- **Color A:** Fisherman
- **Color B:** Marble Grey

Yardage/Meterage
- **Color A:** 10 (12, 14, 16) yd [9 (11, 13, 15) m]
- **Color B:** 46 (48, 50, 52) yd [42 (44, 46, 48) m]

Hook
- US L (8 mm)

Notions
- Yarn needle
- Scissors

Gauge
- 7.5 sts x 4.5 rows = 4" (10 cm) in dc (blocked)

Finished Measurements
- Sample size is 7/8
- **Standard Sizing** (Narrow option in the Notes)
- **Circumference around your Foot (A):** 9.5" (24 cm)
- **Bottom Heel to the Top of the Cuff (B):** 8.5" (21.5 cm)
- **Length (C):** 10 (10.5, 11.5, 12.5)" [25.5 (26.5, 29, 32) cm]

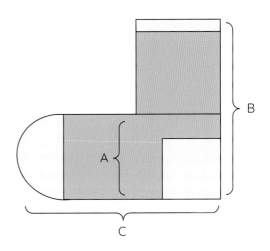

Abbreviations

ch	chain
dc	double crochet
dc2tog	double crochet 2 stitches together
2dc	double crochet twice into the same stitch
hdc	half double crochet
RS	right side
sk	skip
Sl St	slip stitch
st(s)	stitch(es)
WS	wrong side
X Stitch	See Techniques (page 24)

Notes

1. Beginning ch doesn't count as a stitch in this pattern.

2. Meeting gauge will ensure your slipper works up to the size stated. Fits easily over socks.

3. Worked from the toe up.

4. When joining in the round, Sl St into the top of the beginning chain.

5. The entire slipper is seamless and worked in the round, except for the heel which is in rows and sewn up at the end. Use a whip stitch (page 25) for sewing.

6. **How to customize your fit:** If you are between sizes or like a certain amount of snugness for your slipper, you can check your fit when you reach the heel. One row adds 1″ (2.5 cm) in additional length. When you try the slipper on, pinch the last row together and add an extra row or remove a row as needed.

7. **Narrow foot adjustment:** The circumference around your foot is 8.5″ (21.5 cm). If you would like to make a narrower version of this slipper for a snug fit, adjust as follows: dc8 into your magic circle (page 17). Continue to follow the rest of the instructions but remember your stitch counts will be 2 less for every round up to the Heel. Your Heel stitches will be 10, with your Heel Row 4 being: Ch2, turn, dc1, hdc2, sc4, hdc2, dc1 [10 sts]. Stitch count will remain as stated in the pattern for the Leg Section.

Quick and Cozy Slippers Pattern

Toe

Round 1: (RS) With Color A, make a magic circle, ch2, dc9 into it, Sl St into the top of the beginning ch to join in the round and cinch up your magic circle. [9 sts]

Round 2: Ch2, 2dc for the round, Sl St to join in the round. [18 sts]

Round 3: Ch2, dc for the round, Sl St to join in the round.

Rounds 4-7 (8, 9, 10): With Color B, ch2, dc for the round, Sl St to join in the round.

Heel *Row counts will start over for easy counting.*

Row 1: (RS) With Color A, ch2, dc12. [12 sts]

Rows 2-3: Ch2, turn, dc12.

Note: See Notes to customize your fit before working Row 4.

Row 4: (WS) Ch2, turn, dc2, hdc2, sc4, hdc2, dc2. [12 sts]

Cut yarn, leaving a 10" (25.5 cm) tail.

Turn the slipper inside out. With the RS's facing each other, sew up the back of the heel.

Leg Section

Round 1: (RS) Attach Color B with a ch2 centered at the back of the heel, dc22 around the leg opening, working a dc2 along each row ending and one per live stitch across the instep of the slipper, Sl St to join in the round. [22 sts]

Notes: Add or remove sts for a preferred fit around your leg. Use your seaming tail from the heel section to sew up any gaps that may remain.

Round 2: Ch2, sk1, dc until last 2sts, dc2tog, Sl St to join in the round. [20 sts]

Rounds 3-4: Ch2, X stitch for the round, Sl St to join in the round. [20 sts]

Round 5: With Color A, ch1, hdc for the round, Sl St to join in the round.

Fasten off and weave in the ends.

Voila! You're done! Block your project (see page 27 for more instructions).

AT EASE SLIPPERS

Skill Level: Easy • Project Time: 2–2.5 hours for the pair

I love a pair of slipper socks! Sometimes in fall and winter, one pair of socks just isn't enough for my cold toes. I love to have a pair of homemade goodness ready for when this moment arrives. These were designed to fit easily over a thin pair of socks and for an average width foot. I find these fit well with a wide instep, too. If you need a narrow fit, I've got you covered—follow the instructions in the Notes section.

Size
- Women's 5/6 (7/8, 9/10, 11/12)

Materials

Yarn
- Lion Brand Yarn, Worsted Weight, Wool Ease (80% Acrylic, 20% Wool), 197 yd (180 m), 3 oz (85 g)

Shown in
- **Color A:** Oatmeal
- **Color B:** Natural Heather

Yardage/Meterage
- **Color A:** 61 (63, 65, 67) yd [56 (57, 59, 61) m]
- **Color B:** 150 (152, 154, 156) yd [137 (138, 141, 143) m]

Hook
- US F (3.75 mm)

Notions
- Yarn needle
- Scissors

Gauge
- 17 sts X 9.5 row = 4" (10 cm) in dc (blocked)

Finished Measurements
- Sample size is 7/8
- **Standard Sizing** (Narrow option in the Notes)
- **Circumference around your Foot (A):** 8.5" (21.5 cm)
- **Bottom Heel to the Top of the Cuff (B):** 8.5" (21.5 cm)
- **Length (C):** 9 (9.5, 10, 10.5)" [23 (24, 25.5, 26.5 cm)]

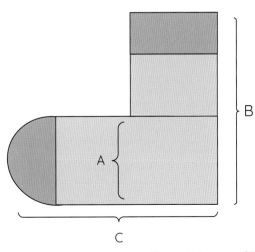

Abbreviations

ch	chain
dc	double crochet
2dc	double crochet twice into the same stitch
hdc	half double crochet
RS	right side
sc	single crochet
sk	skip
Sl St	slip stitch
st(s)	stitches

Notes

1. Beginning ch doesn't count as a stitch in this pattern.

2. The entire slipper is seamless, worked in the round, except for the heel section, which is worked in rows and sewn up at the end. Use a whip stitch (page 25) for sewing.

3. When joining in the round, Sl St into the top of the beginning ch to join in the round.

4. How to customize your fit: If you're between sizes or like a certain amount of snugness for your slipper, you can check your fit when you reach the heel. The Final Heel Row adds $1/2''$ (1 cm) in additional length. When you try the slipper on, pinch the last row together and add an extra row or remove a row as needed.

5. I cut my yarn between color changes.

6. **Narrow foot adjustment:** The circumference around your foot is 7" (18 cm). If you would like to make a narrower version of this slipper for a snug fit, adjust as follows: dc10 into your magic circle (page 17). Continue to follow the rest of the instructions but remember your stitch counts will go up 5 sts for every increase round, ending at 30 sts for Round 5. Your Heel stitch count will be 24, with your Heel Row 7 being: Ch2, turn, dc8, hdc3, sc2, hdc3, dc8 [24 sts]. Stitch count for the Leg Section is 34.

At Ease Slippers Pattern

Toe

Round 1: With Color A, make a magic circle, ch2, dc12 into it, Sl St to join in the round, cinch your magic circle. [12 sts]

Round 2: Ch2, *dc1, 2dc, repeat after * for the round, Sl St to join in the round. [18 sts]

Round 3: Ch2, *dc2, 2dc, repeat after * for the round, Sl St to join in the round. [24 sts]

Round 4: Ch2, *dc3, 2dc, repeat after * for the round, Sl St to join in the round. [30 sts]

Round 5: Ch2, *dc4, 2dc, repeat after * for the round, Sl St to join in the round. [36 sts]

Round 6: Ch2, dc for the round, Sl St to join in the round.

Rounds 7–14 (15, 17, 18): With Color B, ch2, dc for the round, Sl St to join in the round.

Heel *Row counts will start over for easy counting.*

Row 1: Ch2, dc28. [28 sts]

Rows 2–6: Ch2, turn, dc28.

> **Note:** See Notes on page 94 to customize your fit before working Row 7.

Row 7: Ch2, turn, dc10, hdc3, sc2, hdc3, dc10.

Cut yarn, leaving a 10" (25 cm) tail for seaming.

Turn the slipper inside out. RS facing each other, sew up the back of the heel.

Leg Section

Round 1: (RS) Attach Color B with a ch2 centered at the back of the heel, dc36 around the leg opening working a dc2 along each row ending and one per live stitch across the instep of the slipper, Sl St to join in the round. [36 sts]

> **Notes:** Add or remove sts for a preferred fit around your leg. Use your seaming tail from the heel section to sew up any gaps that may remain.

Rounds 2-7: Ch2, dc for the round, Sl St to join in the round.

Round 8: With Color A, ch1, *sk1, (sc1, dc1) in the next stitch, repeat after * for the round, Sl St to join in the round.

Rounds 9-11: Ch2, dc for the round, Sl St to join in the round.

Round 12: With Color B, repeat Round 8.

Fasten off and weave in the ends.

Voila! You're done! Block your project (see page 27 for more instructions).

SUZETTE DISHCLOTH

Skill Level: Basic • Project Time: Small—40 minutes • Medium—1 hour • Large—2 hours

This pattern utilizes the Suzette stitch for stunning, textured cloths that are the perfect addition for any kitchen. I simply love how this stitch works up so easily yet is so full of texture. It's one of my favorite stitches because it doesn't look like a beginner stitch and still looks beautiful no matter what skill level you are at! The best part is that you can work these customizable cloths up in three different sizes and use them as a coaster, pot holder or dishcloth, depending on your needs. Whichever version you choose to make, each one is designed to complement your beautiful kitchen, and guests are sure to notice.

Sizes

- S (M, L)

Materials

Yarn

- Lion Brand Yarn, Worsted Weight, 24/7 Cotton (100% Mercerized Cotton), 186 yd (170 m), 3.5 oz (100 g)

Shown in

- White
- Silver

Yardage/Meterage

- 35 (50, 130) yd [32 (46, 119) m]

Hook

- US H (5 mm)

Notions

- Yarn needle
- Scissors

Gauge

- 14 sts x 13 rows = 4" (10 cm) in Suzette stitch [sk1, (sc1, dc1) in the next stitch] (blocked)

Finished Measurements

- **Length (A):** 5.5 (7.5, 11.5)" [14.5 (18.5, 29) cm]
- **Width (B):** 5 (6, 10.5)" [12.5 (15, 26.5) cm]

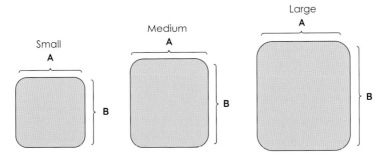

Small
A
B

Medium
A
B

Large
A
B

Abbreviations

ch	chain
dc	double crochet
hdc	half double crochet
sk	skip
RS	right side
st(s)	stitch(es)
sc	single crochet
Sl St	slip stitch
WS	wrong side

Notes

1. Beginning chain doesn't count as a stitch.

2. The starting chain is also referred to as the foundation chain in the pattern.

3. When joining in the round, Sl St into the top of the beginning chain.

4. For this pattern the small size is perfect as a coaster, medium as a trivet or pot holder and the large as a dishcloth.

5. A hdc border is added at the end for a finishing detail.

Suzette Dishcloth Pattern

Dishcloth Ch20 (26, 40).

Row 1: (RS) Starting in the 3rd ch from the hook, sc18 (24, 38). [18 (24, 38) sts]

Rows 2–14 (18, 32): Ch1, turn, *sk1, (sc1, dc1) in the next stitch, repeat after * for the row.

Note: Last row worked is a WS row. Do not cut the yarn; continue to make the border.

Hdc Edging (RS) Ch1, turn, hdc for the row, in the corner (hdc1, ch1, hdc1) for an increase to help it lay flat as the edging curves around the corner (see Photo A), hdc down the side edge (hdc1 per row ending) until the corner, (hdc1, ch1, hdc1) in the corner, hdc1 per stitch along the foundation chain edge, (hdc1, ch1, hdc1) in the corner, hdc down the side edge (hdc1 per row ending), (hdc1, ch1, hdc1) in the corner and Sl St to join in the round to complete your edging.

Fasten off and weave in the ends.

Voila! You're done! Block your project (see page 27 for more instructions).

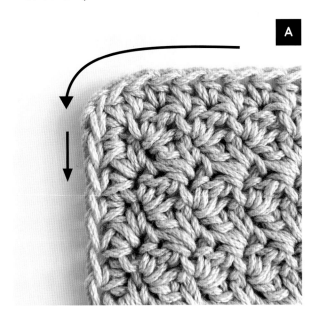

A

OUT + ABOUT ACCESSORIES

From the Willow Basket (page 119) to the Adventurer Backpack (page 105), this section has so many cute on-the-go accessories that work up in just a few hours. And since they're made so quickly, these cute designs would also make amazing gifts! Perfect for a day at the office or out on a hike, you can take your craftsmanship everywhere you go!

ADVENTURER BACKPACK

Skill Level: Easy • Project Time: 4–5 hours

Often when I think about my grandad, I remember him going for long walks as he strolled through beautiful English hillsides, just taking in the day's beauty. From him, I learned that an adventure can be just a few moments away! This backpack is worked up quickly in a bulky yarn for a sturdy structure, and the bag straps are adjustable in length with a single crochet border worked around them to reinforce their strength. The handles for the bag also have a fortifying finishing detail. With this backpack, you'll have plenty of room for any trinkets or flowers you may find on your next adventure.

Sizes

- One size

Materials

Yarn

- Lion Brand Yarn, Bulky Weight, Hue + Me (80% Acrylic, 20% Wool), 137 yd (125 m), 4.4 oz (125 g)

Shown in

- Toast

Yardage/Meterage

- 320 yd (293 m)

Hook

- US K (6.5 mm)

Notions

- 1 button, 1" (30 mm)
- 4, 2" (5-cm) safety pins or sewing pins for strap placement
- Stich markers
- Yarn needle
- Scissors

Gauge

- 9.5 sts x 8 rows = 4" (10 cm) in hdc in the round (blocked)

Finished Measurements

- **Length (A):** 9" (23 cm)
- **Depth (B):** 4" (10 cm)
- **Height (C):** 10" (25.5 cm)

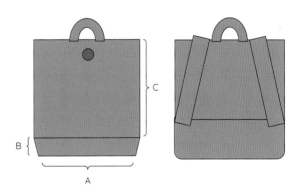

Abbreviations

ch	chain
hdc	half double crochet
M	stitch marker
RS	right side
scblo	single crochet into the back loop of the stitch
sk	skip
sc	single crochet
Sl St	slip stitch
st(s)	stitch(es)
WS	wrong side

Notes

1. Beginning ch doesn't count as a stitch in this pattern.

2. When joining in the round, Sl St into the top of the beginning chain.

3. The bag's body is worked in continuous rounds, like a spiral. This means there's no join followed by a turning chain. Your first stitch of every row is in the first stitch of the previous row.

4. The Purse Straps and Handles are adjustable in length and have a sc border worked around them to reinforce the strength of the straps. The sc border will add a bit of length to all four pieces, and instructions in the pattern will help you to know what length these will be.

Adventurer Backpack Pattern

Base Ch12.

Row 1: (RS) Starting in 3rd ch from the hook, sc10. [10 sts]

Rows 2-26: Ch1, turn, sc10.

Note: Do not cut yarn. Measurements: L 9″ (23 cm) x W 4″ (10 cm)

Backpack Body *Work around the base you just made.*

Round 1: (Photo A) Ch1, turn, sc10, turn left to work down the long side of the rectangle (approx. 1 sc per row ending, making 25 sts), sc1 per foundation ch (10 sts), sc25 down the final long side (25 sts), Sl St to join in the round. [70 sts]

Round 2: (Photo B) Ch1 (no turn), scblo around the base, Sl St to join in the round. [70 sts]

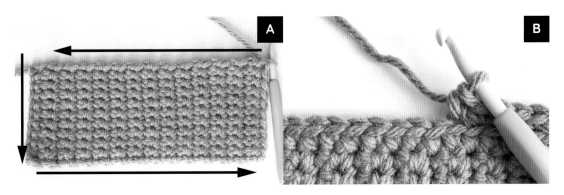

Round 3: Ch2, hdc1, place a M in the first st, hdc for the round.

Note: Instead of Sl St to join in the round at the end, continue to the next round and begin working in continuous rounds or a spiral.

Rounds 4–17: Hdc for the round.

Notes: Each time you come to the stitch with the M (first st of the previous round), replace the M into the newly made stitch to count the new round. At Round 17, the M isn't quite centered but is 2 sts off to one side. In the next round, we will adjust to ensure the button spacing will be centered.

Round 18: Hdc1, replace M, hdc31, ch1, sk1 (buttonhole), hdc for the round. [70 sts]

> **Note:** Due to changes in gauge, you may need to shift where your ch1 goes; just make sure it's centered along this row according to the base of the bag.

Rounds 19-20: Hdc for the round (keep replacing your M).

Round 21: Hdc for the round until 2 sts before the M, sc1, Sl St1, Sl St to join in the round.

Round 22: Beginning in your marked st, Sl St for the round, Sl St to join in the round.

Shoulder Straps *Make two*

Ch4.

Row 1: (RS) Starting in the 2nd ch from hook, sc for the row. [3 sts]

Row 2: Ch1, turn, sc for the row.

> **Note:** Repeat Row 2 until the strap measures 31" (79 cm), or 3" (7.5 cm) short of desired finished length ending on a RS row.

How to Customize the Length Refer to the Attaching Shoulder Straps section (page 110) for strap placement. Use pins to try on the straps and adjust to the desired length. The length will stretch an additional 3" (7.5 cm) in length when the border is added.

Do not cut yarn. Next, we will add a border to reinforce the strap and prevent overstretching.

Strap Border Turning to work along the edges of the strap as we did with the Bag Base, RS still facing you, sc1 per row ending (approximately 90 sts depending on the length of your strap), turn corner and sc3 across short end, turn corner and sc1 per row ending (same number as previous long side), sc3 across short end, Sl St to join in the round.

> **Note:** Each strap will each measure 34" (86 cm) in length when done if you're following my measurements.

Fasten off.

Purse Handles *Make two*

Ch3.

Row 1: Starting in the 2nd ch from the hook, sc for the row. [2 sts]

Rows 2–23: Ch1, turn, sc for the row.

> **Notes:** Each handle measures 8″ (20 cm).
>
> Turn to work a sc edging around the strap as previously done. Fasten off.

Finishing

Button Placement Along the inside, back panel of the bag, mark where your button should be to line up with the buttonhole on the front side of the bag. Using a matching piece of yarn, sew your button along the inside of the backpack. As you sew, make sure your stitches do not show on the RS of the bag. Weave in the ends.

Attaching Purse Handles The RS of the handles get sewn in along the inside of the backpack, one on the front and the other on the back, parallel to each other. The RS of the purse handles should be visible when looking at the RS of the backpack.

Purse Handle Placement (Photo C) Pin the handles centered along the bag, each end 1″ (2.5 cm) down along the inside of the backpack with a 2″ (5 cm) gap between the handle ends. Be careful not to twist them.

The buttonhole on the front side of the bag should be centered along the front handle, and the button along the inside of the backpack should be centered along the back side handle.

(continued)

C

(Photo D) Cut four, 12″ (30.5 cm) lengths of yarn for sewing each end of the straps. Sew the handles so that the stitches don't show on the outside (RS) of the bag. I sewed in a square shape, attaching the handle to the inside of the bag. The WS of the handle should be facing the inside of the bag.

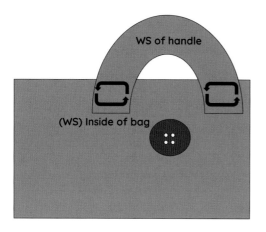

You want the edges flat, and the handles even.

Weave in the ends.

Attaching Shoulder Straps Start with the back of the backpack bag facing you, RS up. Cut four 12″ (30.5 cm) lengths of yarn for sewing each end of the straps to the backpack.

Top of the straps: Pin the RS top 4 rows of the strap centered under the purse handle. Have WS of the strap facing you for sewing.

Bottom of the straps: Pin the bottom edge of the strap where the base meets the backpack body (Round 1), 1 stitch in from each edge of the bag base. Sew along the edge, 6 rows up on the strap to the bag so that it's securely attached.

Weave in the ends.

Voila! You're done! Block your project (see page 27 for more instructions).

MARLO TOTE

Skill Level: Easy • Project Time: 4–5 hours

Who says yarn can't look elegant? Wear this tote out for a fancy dinner or take it to the office, and no one will guess you made it yourself! I love how the combo of this worsted yarn and simple stitch gives this bag a woven texture. This one has all sorts of fun folds and seaming to give your bag tons of character and strength for whatever you store in it. Pair it with any strap or handle to show your own personal flair. Think gift with this one, and your bestie will love you!

Sizes

- One size

Materials

Yarn

- Lion Brand Yarn, Worsted Weight, Wool Ease (80% Acrylic, 20% Wool), 197 yd (180 m), 3 oz (85 g)

Yardage/Meterage

- 315 yd (288 m)

Shown in

- Oatmeal

Hook

- US J (6 mm)

Notions

- Purse straps (Measurements: L 24" [61 cm] x width 5" [12.5 cm])
- Yarn needle
- Scissors

Gauge

- 12 sts x 12 rows = 4" (10 cm) in hdc between the st posts (blocked)

Finished Measurements

- **Width (A):** 15.5" (39.5 cm)
- **Height (B):** 15.5" (39.5 cm) without strap
- **Rectangle before seaming:** 10.5" (26.5 cm) x 32" (81 cm)

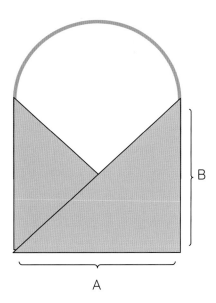

Abbreviations

ch	chain
hdc	half double crochet
RS	right side
sc	single crochet
2sc	single crochet twice into the same stitch
Sl St	slip stitch
st(s)	stitch(es)
WS	wrong side

Notes

1. Beginning ch doesn't count as a stitch in this pattern.

2. Your starting chain is referred to as your foundation chain throughout the pattern.

3. When joining in the round, Sl St into the top of the beginning chain.

4. The hdcs are worked between the stitch posts for the pattern.

5. The bag is worked up in a rectangle and then folded and sewn into its final shape. It is finished with a sc edging around the entire thing. It's then folded and seamed into an envelope shape.

Marlo Tote Pattern

Bag Ch34.

Row 1: (RS) Starting in the 3rd ch from the hook, hdc32. [32 sts]

Rows 2-96: Ch1, turn, hdc between the st posts for the row.

Note: Last row is a WS row.

Do not cut yarn; continue to Sc Edging.

Sc Edging (RS) Ch1, turn, sc for the row, in the corner sc1 again for an increase to help it lay flat as the edging curves around the corner, sc down the side edge (sc1 per row ending) until the corner, 2sc in the corner, sc1 per stitch along the foundation chain edge, 2sc in the corner, sc down the side edge (sc1 per row ending), 2sc in the corner and Sl St to join in the round to complete your edging. [260 sts]

Fasten off and weave in the ends.

Seaming Use a slip stitch seam. Lay the rectangle down (WS up) in front of you, lengthwise, with the foundation chain at the left and the last row worked at your right.

Step 1: (Diagram A) Fold the bottom left corner up to the rectangle edge. The foundation ch row is now lined up along the long side edge.

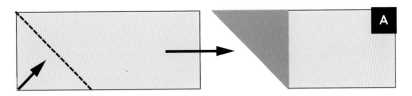

Step 2: (Diagram B) Take the bottom right corner and fold it up. The bottom edge now meets the edge we just folded, forming a point.

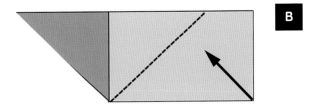

Step 3: (Photos C and D) Seam the two edges together (working through both loops of the stitches), starting at the bottom point of the bag and working up to the center of the bag (Diagram E). Fasten off.

Step 4: Turn the bag over to continue folding.

Step 5: Now fold the last pointed section into the center of the bag.

Step 6: Seam up the two edges like you did previously. Fasten off.

Attaching Your Purse Straps

I used a pair of straps I found at my local craft store that had rings at each end for an easy placement. I recommend visiting my Amazon storefront (link on my website, whistleandwool.com) for a few good substitution options if you can't find some locally.

See Photo F for the approximate placement. Place the ring of the strap 1" (2.5 cm) down on the corner point. Adjust as needed according to your own straps and preferences (Photos G and H). Fold the corner over and seam the strap end to the bag to secure.

Repeat for both sides and weave in any remaining ends.

Voila! You're done! Block your project (see page 27 for more instructions).

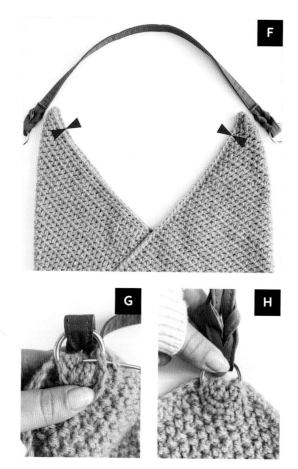

WILLOW BASKET

Skill Level: Easy • Project Time: 3 hours

Whether you're out wandering through fallen golden leaves on a fall day, strolling through a meadow on a spring morning or shell picking on the beach during a sunny summer day, this basket was made with the idea of fun and whimsical moments along the way! In just a few short hours and with two skeins of bulky yarn, you can work up this adorable basket. With multiple stitches used to create a textured look, this fun and functional basket also has rolled handles for stability and to elevate its simple construction.

Sizes
- One size

Materials

Yarn
- Lion Brand Yarn, Bulky Weight, Hue + Me (80% Acrylic, 20% Wool), 137 yd (125 m), 4.4 oz (125 g)

Shown in
- Artichoke

Yardage/Meterage
- 202 yd (185 m)

Hook
- US K (6.5 mm)

Notions
- Scissors
- Yarn needle
- Pins

Gauge
- 10.5 sts x 5.5 rows = 4" (10 cm) (blocked) in X stitch (page 24)

Finished Measurements
- **Width (A):** 13.5" (34 cm)
- **Height (B):** 14.5" (37 cm)

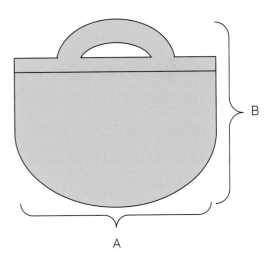

Abbreviations

ch	chain
hdc	half double crochet
2hdc	half double crochet twice into the same stitch
sc	single crochet
sk	skip
Sl St	slip stitch
X Stitch	See Techniques (page 24)

Notes

1. Beginning ch doesn't count as a stitch in this pattern.

2. The bag is worked in the round from the bottom up, and the rounded handle detail is sewn into place at the end.

3. When joining in the round, Sl St into the top of the beginning chain.

Willow Basket Pattern

Basket

Round 1: Beginning with a magic circle (page 17), ch2 and hdc10 into it, Sl St to join in the round. [10 sts]

Round 2: Ch2, 2hdc into each stitch, Sl st to join in the round. [20 sts]

Round 3: Ch2, *hdc1, 2hdc, repeat after * for the round, Sl St to join in the round. [30 sts]

Round 4: Ch2, *hdc2, 2hdc, repeat after * for the round, Sl St to join in the round. [40 sts]

Round 5: Ch2, *hdc3, 2hdc, repeat after * for the round, Sl St to join in the round. [50 sts]

Round 6: Ch2, *hdc4, 2hdc, repeat after * for the round, Sl St to join in the round. [60 sts]

Round 7: Ch2, *hdc5, 2hdc, repeat after * for the round, Sl St to join in the round. [70 sts]

Rounds 8–9: Ch2, hdc for the round, Sl St to join in the round.

Rounds 10–18: Ch2, X stitch for the round, Sl St to join in the round.

Round 19: Ch2, hdc for the round, Sl St to join in the round.

Round 20: Ch1, sc for the round, Sl St to join in the round.

Handles

Round 1: Ch1, sc10, sk15, ch25 (for the handle), sc20, sk15, ch25 (second handle), sc10, Sl St to join in the round. [40 sc, 90 sts, including chains]

Rounds 2–5: Ch1, sc for the round (working into the chains as you come to them), Sl St to join in the round. [90 sts]

Fasten off, leaving a tail two times the circumference of the bag.

Finishing

For this section, we will fold over the entire rim of the bag (the last round worked) along the inside of the bag. This will add durability and a finished rolled look to the top of the bag and handles (Photo A).

Take the last round of the Handles and fold it over so that the edge lines up with the chain row when you were creating the Handle sections (Photo B). This depth is very important. It will be the depth you follow for the entire rim of the bag.

Pin the edge in place along the entire inside of the bag to make sure it stays aligned as you sew.

Using your long tail end, thread your yarn needle.

Sew the last round worked down along the inside of the bag. Make sure your stitches don't show on the RS of the bag. Once you reach the handle, whip stitch the two edges together (Photo C) to create a circular shape for the Handle (ch edge is stitched to the edge of the last round worked). Continue going around the entire bag (Photo D), completing your second Handle and going back to where you started.

Weave in the ends.

Voila! You're done! Block your project (see page 27 for more instructions).

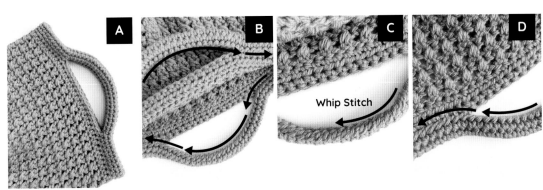

Whip Stitch

CAPE COWL AND HAT SET

Skill Level: Basic • Project Time: 3-4 hours for the set

This set was fun to design and was a brilliant stash buster. Sometimes we need quick but cute ideas to help use up those lonely skeins left over from other projects. And in under four hours, this can be yours. When working up other designs for the book, like the Shelter Shawl (page 63), don't toss your yarn. Make this cozy set like I did. I have always loved a yellow and blue combo, and this color combination mixed with stripes creates a nautical and sunshine-yellow sea vibe. With a mini shawl shape to the cowl, it adds some coziness around your neck as you tackle the day!

Sizes

- One size

Materials

Yarn

- Lion Brand Yarn, Bulky Weight, Hue + Me (80% Acrylic, 20% Wool), 137 yds (125 m), 4.4 oz (125 g)

Shown in

- **Color A:** Mustard
- **Color B:** Whisper
- **Color C:** Magic Hour

Yardage/Meterage

- **Cowl:** 203 yd (186 m)
- **Hat:** 93 yd (85 m)

Hooks

- US M (9 mm)

Notions

- 1 toggle button [Organics Elements, Coconut 1.5" (4 cm)]
- Yarn needle
- Scissors

Gauge

- 7 sts x 7 rows = 4" (10 cm) in hdc between the st posts (blocked)

Finished Measurements

Cowl:

- **Length (A):** 40" (101.5 cm)
- **Width (widest point) (B):** 20" (51 cm)

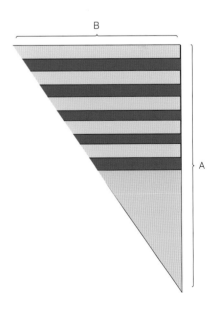

Hat:
- **Circumference:** (C) 23" (58.5 cm)
- **Height:** (D) 8.5" (21.5 cm)

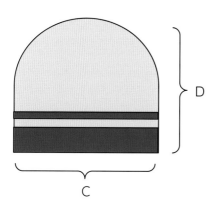

Abbreviations

ch	chain
hdc	half double crochet
2hdc	half double crochet twice into the same stitch
RS	right side
sc	single crochet
Sl St	slip stitch
st(s)	stitch(es)
WS	wrong side

Notes

1. Beginning ch doesn't count as a stitch in this pattern.

2. Your last "between the stitch post" for the row gets worked between the last post and turning ch from the previous row.

3. The number of chains in the turning chain alternates from RS to WS to help form the triangular shape and keep the edges stretchy.

4. When joining in the round, Sl St into the top of the beginning chain.

5. The Cowl is worked from the bottom up, beginning at the point. The hat is worked in the round and is seamless.

6. All hdcs throughout the pattern are worked between the st posts.

7. **Hat Sizing:** To make a Child/Adult Small hat [20" (51 cm)] match gauge, and then go one hook size down to work the pattern as stated.

Cape Cowl and Hat Set Pattern

Cowl With Color A, ch3.

Row 1: (RS) Starting in the 3rd ch from the hook, hdc1. [1 st]

Row 2: (WS) Ch2, turn, hdc between the st post and the previous rows starting ch.

Row 3: Ch2, turn, 2hdc between the st post and the previous rows starting ch. [2 sts]

Row 4: Ch3, turn, hdc between the st posts for the row.

Row 5: Ch2, turn, hdc between the st posts until the last st, 2hdc between the st posts. [3 sts]

Row 6: Ch3, turn, hdc between the st posts for the row.

Rows 7–52: Repeat Rows 5 and 6. [26 sts]

Rows 53–54: With Color B, repeat Rows 5 and 6. [27 sts]

Note: I cut my yarn between color changes and crocheted over my ends to weave them in as I went.

Rows 55–56: With Color C, repeat Rows 5 and 6. [28 sts]

Rows 57–70: Repeat Rows 53–56, continuing to switch colors every 2 rows, ending on a Color B section. [35 sts]

Fasten off and weave in the ends.

Button Fastening Lay your Cowl down with the RS facing you. With Color A, sew your button along the middle of Row 65 to match the sample shown or adjust to your own preference. Wrap your cowl around your neck and push the button between the stitches around Row 14 on the Color A section of the Cowl for a bit of ruffle and depth, as pictured.

Hat

Round 1: With Color B, make a magic circle (page 17), ch2, hdc 8 into it, Sl St to join in the round. Cinch up your magic circle. [8 sts]

Round 2: Ch1, working between the st posts for the round, 2hdc into each stitch, Sl St to join in the round. [16 sts]

Round 3: (Photo A) Ch1, working between the st posts for the round, *hdc1, 2hdc, repeat after the * for the round, Sl St to join in the round. [24 sts]

All of your 2hdcs will fall between the 2sts increased on the previous rounds.

Round 4: Ch1, working between the st posts for the round, *hdc2, 2hdc, repeat after the * for the round, Sl St to join in the round. [32 sts]

Round 5: Ch1, *working between the st posts for the round, hdc3, 2hdc, repeat after the * for the round, Sl St to join in the round. [40 sts]

Note: The diameter measures 7.5" (18.5 cm) across.

Rounds 6–10: With Color B, ch1, hdc between the st posts for the round, Sl St to join in the round. [40 sts]

Round 11: With Color C, repeat Round 10.

Round 12: With Color B, repeat Round 10.

Rounds 13–15: With Color C, repeat Round 10.

Round 16: Ch1, sc for the round, Sl St to join in the round.

Fasten off and weave in the ends.

Voila! You're done! Block your project (see page 27 for more instructions).

BREEZY HEADBAND

Skill Level: Easy • Project Time: 1.5 hours

A soft and cozy headband to keep your ears toasty warm! This one works up like a breeze and keeps you cozy as you go about your day. After a morning of stitching, you could be out and about looking as cute as can be with this special twisty topper. I love the way the detailed knot plays off the classic linen texture on the band. The timeless style will get you through every season.

Sizes

- One size

Materials

Yarn

- Lion Brand Yarn, Worsted Weight, Chainette (70% Alpaca, 18% Virgin Wool, 12% Polyamide), 1.75 oz (50 g)

Shown in

- Beige

Yardage/Meterage

- 105 yd (96 m)

Hook

- US J (6 mm)

Notions

- Yarn needle
- Scissors

Gauge

- 19 sts x 17 rows = 4" (10 cm) (blocked) in linen stitch (page 21) (Row 2 in pattern repeated)

Finished Measurements

- **For reference:** Model is wearing 21" (53 cm) headband with 1" (2.5 cm) of negative ease
- **Length (A):** 10.5" (26.5 cm), when seamed
- **Width (B):** 5" (12.5 cm)

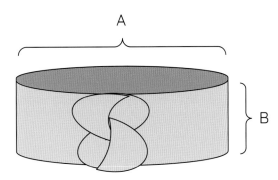

Abbreviations

ch(s) chain(s)

RS right side

sc single crochet

sk skip

st(s) stitch(es)

WS wrong side

Notes

1. Beginning ch doesn't count as a stitch in this pattern, so when we "ch1, sk1," we are skipping the stitch at the base of the turning ch and working our first sc into the stitch next to it.

2. The starting chain is referred to as a foundation chain in the pattern.

3. The headband is worked in two pieces. A smaller piece is wrapped around the band and seamed to create a faux knot look.

4. Use a whip stitch method (page 25) to sew your headband.

Breezy Headband Pattern

Headband Ch24.

Row 1: (RS) Starting in the 4th ch from the hook, sc1, *ch1, sk1, sc1, repeat after the * for the row. [22 sts]

Rows 2–89: Ch1, turn, *ch1, sk1, sc1, repeat after * for the row. [22 sts]

Notes: Measures 21" (53 cm) in length.

You can adjust this to any length by adding or removing rows. Every 4 rows would add or remove 1" (2.5 cm) in length.

Fasten off.

Faux Knot Ch13.

Row 1: (RS) Starting in the 2nd ch from the hook, sc for the row. [12 sts]

Rows 2–25: Ch1, turn, sc for the row.

Fasten off and leave a 10" (25.5 cm) tail for seaming the short ends together.

Seaming the Headband With the RS facing you, bring the two short ends together (foundation ch and the last row worked).

With the WS now facing you, sew the ends together.

Seaming the Faux Knot Piece Onto the Headband

(Photo A) Lay your headband down, vertically, RS up. Insert the faux knot shorter piece horizontally through the center of the headband, RS up.

Bring the short ends of the faux knot together so that it's wrapped around one side of the headband.

(Photo B) With the RSs of the faux knot facing each other, overlap the ends halfway across each other and fold the ends in. It forms an S shape with the edges.

(Photos C, D and E) Seam all four edges together. Seam them together in one direction, and then go back again in the opposite direction to make sure you've seamed all edges.

Weave in your ends and turn the seamed faux knot right side out. Place the tie section over the Headband seam to make it look seamless (Photo F).

Optional: Tack sew it on the underneath side so that the tie section doesn't move along the headband.

Voila! You're done! Block your project (see page 27 for more instructions).

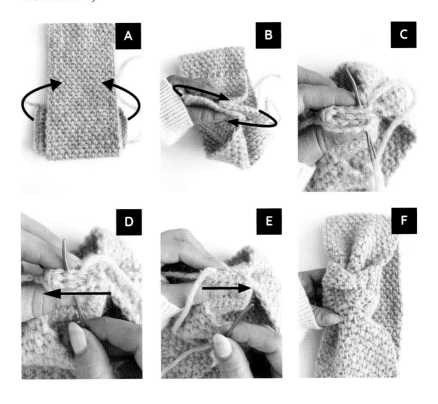

CASCADE BOW

Skill Level: Easy • Project Time: 2–2.5 hours

A hair accessory like this takes your style from everyday to gorgeous. With its added length, you can easily pull your hair half-back or up in a cute pony-tail and allow this bow to cascade dreamily down your hair. Worked up in a DK yarn and soft merino wool, this pattern also has an added softness and was designed to be gentle on your hair. Quick and easy to make, you can be done by the time you've finished a movie and it makes an amazing gift.

Sizes
- One size

Materials

Yarn
- Lion Brand Yarn, DK Weight, LB Collection Superwash Merino (100% Extra Fine Wool), 306 yd (280 m), 3.5 oz (100 g)

Yardage/Meterage
- 109 yd (100 m)

Shown in
- Quail

Hook
- US H (5mm)

Notions
- Yarn needle
- Scissors

Gauge
- 16 sts x 17 rows = 4" (10 cm) in hdc between the st posts (blocked)

Finished Measurements
- **Length (A)** 20" (51 cm)
- **Width (B):** 3.5" (9 cm)

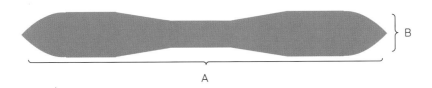

A

B

Abbreviations

ch	chain
hdc	half double crochet
2hdc	half double crochet twice into the same stitch
hdc2tog	half double crochet 2 stitches together
RS	right side
st(s)	stitch(es)
WS	wrong side

Notes

1. Beginning chain doesn't count as a stitch.
2. When joining in the round, Sl St into the top of the beginning chain.
3. The bow is worked in one piece with shaping throughout it.
4. All stitches throughout the pattern are worked in between the stitch posts.
5. Your last "between the stitch post" for the row gets worked between the last post and turning ch from the previous row.

Cascade Bow Pattern

Bow Ch3.

Row 1: (RS) In the 3rd ch from the hook, hdc1. [1 st]

Row 2: Ch2, turn, 2hdc between the st posts (between the previous rows turning ch and hdc). [2 sts]

Row 3: Ch2, turn, 2hdc between the st posts for the row. [4 sts]

Note: (Photo A) All stitches throughout the remaining pattern are worked between the stitch posts.

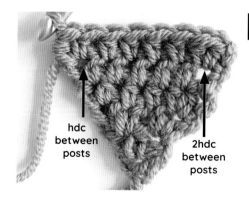

A

hdc between posts

2hdc between posts

Row 4: Ch2, turn, 2hdc between the st posts, hdc between the st posts until the last st, 2hdc between the st posts. [6 sts]

Row 5: Ch2, turn, hdc between the st posts for the row.

Rows 6-10: Repeat Rows 4 and 5, end with a Row 4 repeat. [12 sts]

Straight section

Rows 11-26: Repeat Row 5.

Decrease section

Row 27: (RS) Ch2, turn, hdc2tog between the st posts, hdc between the st posts until the last 2 sts, hdc2tog between the st posts. [10 sts]

Rows 28-30: Repeat Row 5.

Row 31: Repeat Row 27. [8 sts]

Center section

Rows 32-52: Repeat Row 5.

Increase section

Row 53: (RS) Repeat Row 4. [10 sts]

Rows 54-56: Repeat Row 5.

Row 57: Repeat Row 4. [12 sts]

Straight section

Rows 58-74: Repeat Row 5.

Decrease section

Row 75: (RS) Repeat Row 27. [10 sts]

Row 76: Repeat Row 5.

Rows 77-80: Repeat Rows 75 and 76. [6 sts]

Rows 81-82: Repeat Row 27. [2 sts]

Row 83: Ch2, turn, hdc2tog between the st posts. [1 st]

Note: Do not cut yarn; continue to Edging.

Edging (RS) Ch1, working along the outside of the bow, sc around.

Make sc1 per row ending, adjusting as needed to ensure that your edging lays flat. If it buckles, you have too many sts; if it pulls tight, you have too few.

When you return to the beginning of the round, Sl St to join in the round.

Fasten off and weave in the ends.

Voila! You're done! Block your project (see page 27 for more instructions).

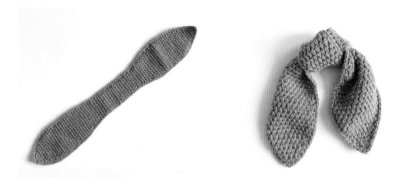

This is what your finished piece will look like.

THANK YOU HUGS!

Family

To my lovely Gran, thank you for teaching me your love for yarn so early on in my life. I remember that rainy summer day in England like it was yesterday. My love for knitting, crocheting and creating new things only grew from there. I wish you could see all the things I've made since then.

To my amazing husband and kids, your constant support as I designed non-stop all summer with the dream of putting together this book was everything. Every time you saw me with yarn swirling all around and taking yarn just about everywhere we went, you always encouraged me and made me feel like my creative energy was just where it was supposed to be. Stephen, you're always the best, but surprising me with a large PSL (my favorite) on days you knew I had hours of work ahead was just next level. You truly are my supportive knight in shining armor!

Thanks Mum! Over the years, you always shared your (and Gran's) tips and tricks for knitting and crocheting, and I'm so glad you did. Through all the years, it's still my favorite thing, and I love that we share the joy of it.

Thank you, Dad! You always taught me not to be scared to try something new, and I know that lesson gave me the added courage to create this book. It's a leap I'll always be so glad I took.

To my big bros, from proofreading tips to helping me get my photography set up, thank you for always being so supportive.

To my hub's family, who always checked in with me for exciting book updates and always had confidence that it would turn out great—Mark, Arlene and Nana—it meant so much, thank you!

Thank you to all my friends who supported me throughout this process when I needed it. A special thank you to the Kowalskis and Corbins for opening your homes to add to my "cozy at home" and "relaxing days at the beach" vibes with my photos. I'm so excited I get to share this with all of you now!

And a special thank you to all of you for your kindness and support of my book. I hope you love all the cozy things you make and don't forget to join me on Instagram— let's be yarn friends :)

Page Street Publishing

Thank you so much to Emily for reaching out to me for this wonderful opportunity to team up with Page Street Publishing and getting this process started. Thank you so much to Erica for being an amazing editor, who saw me through this whole process and helped make this all I dreamt it would be. And to Laura Benton, thank you so much for all your design work and helping me make this book's layout feel like me, bringing my photos and patterns to life.

Yarn

A big shout out and thanks to Lion Brand Yarn and Mark McCowan for all of the amazing yarn support you see throughout the book. I remember Vanna's Choice and Wool Ease being some of the first yarns I used as a kid when I knit with my mum. It felt like a full-circle moment using this yarn to create all of the patterns for my first book.

Tech Editors

Thank you so much to my awesome Pattern Tech Editors, Nicky Jenson and Erin Battle! Thank you so much for helping me get everything perfect throughout the book with these cozy patterns, poring over everything row by row with me—phew, we did it!

Tester Love!

The superheroes of this project. I say superheroes because you all caught the pesky typos that snuck past me and freed up your time to sometimes work on quite a few of the book patterns over the course of months. You're beyond awesome!! Thank you, thank you, thank you Lo Shapera, Becky Flannery, Jo-Anne Schmid, Lizzie Jones, Alice Van-Sant, Kimmie Walker, Suzanne Casavant, Helen Manzo, Vanessa Coscarelli Black, Anae Cotton and Lynette Stone.

ABOUT *the* AUTHOR

Angie Bivins is the designer and creator behind Whistle and Wool. She loves to design anything that brings an added dose of cozy to the everyday. As a busy mama, she is often multitasking throughout the day, so working on a relaxing project that's easy to set down and pick up, while knowing exactly where you left off, is the inspiration behind each and every design. Making sure projects have a relaxing quality and feel from start to finish is essential. If she's not winding down with her yarn, creating something new or hanging out with her family, you can often find her playing a game of tennis with her husband!

INDEX